# Shifting Sands:
## The People Side of Project Management

*To Wei Wu,
Thanks for wanting to build people skills — good luck!*

*Jana*

# Shifting Sands:
## The People Side of Project Management
**Jana Markowitz and William Berghel**

Jana Markowitz and William Berghel
2013

Copyright © 2013 by Jana Markowitz and William Berghel

All rights reserved. This book or any portion thereof may not be reproduced or used in any manner whatsoever without the express written permission of the publisher except for the use of brief quotations in a book review or scholarly journal.

First Printing: 2013

ISBN 978-1-304-40953-9

Jana Markowitz and William Berghel
5305 N Clover Drive
Memphis, TN 38120

www.shiftingsandsprojectmanagement.com

# Contents

Foreword ............................................................................. vii

Introduction ........................................................................ 1

Chapter 1: Planning Your Project ............................................. 3

Chapter 2: Credibility and Influencing ..................................... 14

Chapter 3: Organizational Change Management and Communications ................................................................. 27

Chapter 4: Conflict Resolution, Issue Resolution and Coping with Resistance ........................................................ 41

Chapter 5: Risk Management ................................................ 57

Chapter 6: Metrics ............................................................... 65

Chapter 7: Don't Go It Alone ................................................. 73

Appendix A ........................................................................ 82

Appendix B ........................................................................ 83

# Foreword

With over forty years of combined project experience, we've handled well-defined projects and chaotic projects on the verge of mutiny; big projects and small projects; projects with short timelines and projects that lasted years; projects that had their scope increased, and projects that had their budgets cut.

Our projects have ranged from IT infrastructure projects, network implementations, and outsourcing engagements to automation and enterprise IT projects. All were successful. Of the various software-development projects, over 80% were delivered on time, none was more than three weeks late, and all were delivered within budget.

Why did these projects succeed? And why aren't all project managers achieving similar results?

Project managers are taught to plan and deliver projects in a world of solid ground. But what they find when they step into the real world is shifting sand. Inadequately prepared for this dynamic environment, they often lose their footing as they encounter unanticipated situations. That's why we have written this book.

For decades the Gartner Group has assured us that, "of IT projects that fail, about 70% fail for non-technical reasons." In our experience the number is closer to 100%. We have never seen a project fail for technical reasons alone.

At the end of the day, projects are groups of people working toward a common goal. The key phrase here is *groups of people*. Psychology teaches that people behave in somewhat predictable ways. Armed with the proper people skills, you can turn a failing project around, or better yet, prevent it from failing in the first place. By paying attention to the "people side" of project management, you will be able to overcome issues, resolve conflicts, create happy customers and walk confidently on the ever-shifting sand.

Jana and Bill
Memphis, Tennessee

# Introduction

This book focuses on the people skills needed to master the critical aspects of project management. We wrote this book with a broad audience in mind. We not only see this as a book for both new and experienced project managers, but also as a resource for project team members, sponsors and other stakeholders to make participating in corporate projects less painful.

One could also use this book to understand why projects fail and to learn how to apply people skills in specific situations to help future projects succeed. This book is both diagnostic ("what does having this type of problem tell me?") and prescriptive ("do these things to prevent these sorts of problems?").

Project management is traditionally taught as structured phases and processes with only a tip of the hat to "soft skills." There is an assumption that the project manager has complete control over all timing, resources, constraints and actions associated with the project. While all of the structure—tasks, deliverables, metrics, reporting—is certainly necessary in order to plan and run a project, it is not sufficient by itself. The "people side" of the equation is essential. Project managers *must* know-how to establish their credibility, manage conflict, satisfy stakeholders, resolve issues and influence behaviors.

After careful analysis we found there is not a one-to-one correspondence between project phases and specific people skills. Any people skill might come into play during any phase. While some chapters and topics will naturally apply more during certain project phases, all chapters include information which is applicable throughout the project timeline.

Therefore these chapters do not have to be read consecutively, although occasionally one chapter may refer to a previous chapter. All chapters conclude with a list of Key Lessons to reiterate critical concepts.

Jana Markowitz and William Berghel

# Chapter 1: Planning Your Project

We once worked in an environment where the enemy was not our competitor, but our own Finance, Legal, and Human Resources departments. These groups always said "no" or otherwise tried to place roadblocks in front of projects. This was doubly so for Information Technology software projects.

Over the years, our organization had developed an informal "best practice" of hiding all IT projects from Finance and Legal as long as possible. These two groups would eventually be brought in just prior to the release date. Executive officers would get involved, decisions would be overruled, feelings would be hurt, hands would be slapped—but the projects were usually allowed to proceed, if somewhat reluctantly.

Our project was similar. We wanted to spend money during one of those periods when funding was scarce, yet we had no hard return on investment. We wanted to roll out a product with sensitive data when Legal was clamping down on such projects. And our IT Operations group was not going to be happy to find that every major component for our proposed deliverable required exceptions to their standards.

We had barely started the project, yet it was already slipping through our fingers. There was no way we could overcome these hurdles at the end of our project.

So we tried something different.

**Chapter Summary**

This chapter is not intended as a substitute for learning project planning basics. It is intended to help novice project managers who are uncertain about how the steps they have heard in class or read in a book should look in the real world.

Shifting Sands

This chapter is also beneficial for experienced project managers who have been slammed in previous projects by scope creep, lack of resources and tight timeframes and who would love to prevent these painful experiences in future projects.

Key ideas in this chapter include managing interdependencies, estimating, identifying stakeholders and effectively transitioning projects once they are rolled out.

**Planning**

The beginning of every project is the project plan. Even the project charter is part of the project plan.

The Project Management Institute has much to say about planning a project, so we won't go into much detail here. At a minimum, you want to know the scope of the project (the deliverables, what is changing and what is not changing), the resources required (by type and quantity), and the timeline of the major deliverables. You will then break down the deliverables into smaller and smaller components (the work breakdown structure), then assign those components to individuals or groups and schedule them. You then add a risk management plan, since the original plan never happens quite the way you think it will. And you track progress against that plan.

There are many books, blogs, and people to get you started. Yet because many of the project planning resources assume that the project manager is already experienced, novices often have problems with their first projects. In addition, when working on smaller projects, the project manager often finds that many components recommended by PMI may be more trouble to put into the project plan than they are worth.

In short, the problem is obtaining the right amount of information to put into the plan.

As project managers who have "been there, done that," we recommend focusing on these key components of the project plan:

- Identifying and engaging stakeholders.

- Managing interdependencies among scope, resources and timeline.

- Estimating effectively.

- Rolling out the project.

**Identify and involve stakeholder as early as possible**

Even novice project managers are able to point out the project sponsor or the software developers. They may even be able to find a user. These are all examples of stakeholders, those people who are, or will be, affected by your project in one way or another.

The problem is that many project managers stop when they run out of people who are actively taking part in the project. They ignore the people who don't care about the project, and they label those who oppose the project as troublemakers.

The troublemakers are often excluded from project discussions, even when their input and support is critical to project success. At many companies, the Finance, Legal, and Human Resources departments fall into this group. People avoid them like the plague, trusting that it is better to ask forgiveness than permission.

In response, we urge you to remember the Sun-Tzu adage, "Keep your friends close, but your enemies closer."

If you have funding issues or if you need help crafting your return on investment, your Finance team will be able to help. They can ensure that your business case is solid and that your funding is locked down before you go too far. The benefit to early funding is that you can assure your team of the true priority of the project. Everyone likes to jump on the winner's bandwagon.

If you have special contractual or other legal needs, your Legal team will be able to help ensure that your project—and your company—is protected. Once they understand what you're trying to accomplish, they will work with you to find out the best way for your project to succeed. We have found that engaging Legal early in the project usually means the answer is "yes."

If you have process changes, job-responsibility changes, or new job titles associated with the project, your Human Resources team can help you navigate the complex world of organizational management. Personnel often says "no" not out of spite but because of the long lead times to implement organizational-management action plans. If you ask late, then the answer has to be "no," because there is not enough time for them to develop a solution that allows them to say "yes." A better strategy is to give Human Resources as much time as possible to help you.

Another group that is frequently overlooked is your training group. Whether the training function is part of Human Resources or is handled by a different department, it is essential to engage trainers early because effective training is a critical success factor for any project. This applies to everyone who will be involved in rolling out your project or supporting your users after the go-live date.

As time-consuming, politically tricky or painful as it might be to include some of these groups in the early planning stages, the result is almost always better than the result you would get by leaving them in the dark.

## Managing Interdependencies among Scope, Resources and Timeline

Scope creep. Lack of resources. Mandated timeframes. If you have not experienced these problems, you have not managed a project.

Yet if you look at much of the project management literature, you might mistakenly think that these problems don't exist. Instead all projects begin cleanly: the scope is well-defined, resources are set and committed on day one, and the timeline has been accepted by all parties, from the project sponsor to each team member working on individual tasks. And even when changes are made to scope, resources and timeline, people are given ample notice and plenty of opportunity to consider the adjustments and decide whether they are worth pursuing.

However, when you talk to project managers, even the ones who wrote the project management literature, you will not find any instances of projects that start cleanly and progress according to commonly embraced theory. Instead you often find projects start in the middle and progress in all directions. You find requirements change at the last minute, critical resources are no longer available, and your executive sponsor wants the project six weeks earlier than planned. And, of course, all of these are non-negotiable.

But this is not always bad. Projects today are very fluid, especially IT projects trying to implement deliverables in an "Agile" environment. If you can adapt and be resilient enough to operate in this environment, you will find that your projects succeed where others' fail.

What is a project manager to do? How do you keep the project from spinning out of control? As a project manager you have options:

- Do nothing, insisting instead that the project remain on its original course. The problem with this option is that your sponsor may not be happy, your developers will be scrambling, your project will probably be late and you will drive your team crazy.

- Make many tiny course corrections accommodating the easier changes, but deferring the painful efforts to a future project manager. This approach never fully meets stakeholder expectations, even if it officially meets the project objectives.

- Embrace the reality of having to meet altered stakeholder and sponsor expectations and ever-changing business needs—even if that means you have to re-plan the project, get original project constraints changed or removed, or completely change the timeline.

The key is not to avoid change, but to adjust your project plan accordingly. First, don't panic. Change happens. The trick is to understand the impact of the changes and manage the interdependencies among the scope, resources, and timeline.

In its simplest form a project has three parts: delivery of a certain scope, by a specific date, using a defined set of resources. In a fluid project anything may change as long as the team has flexibility to adjust in other areas.

To see how this plays out, let's consider an example where we have a last-minute requirements change while at the same time losing a critical resource, yet the sponsor wants the project early. With all three components changing, the project manager will need to analyze how each one impacts scope, resources, and timeline to find a way to make it all happen. Do we have flexibility in scope? Can we trade one deliverable for another? When we lose one critical resource, do we have flexibility to add multiple resources to compensate (i.e. can we increase funding or add several people if we lose only one person?) Do all of the project deliverables need to be six weeks early or can we postpone some to get the one critical element delivered sooner? Is funding available if you need to pursue alternative actions?

This is where your stakeholders can save you. Talk to your sponsors, developers, Finance, Legal; brainstorm possible solutions that meet the changed requirements. More often than not, a best solution will present itself.

Once you have this solution, validate with *all* of the stakeholders that it is reasonable and acceptable. Ensure that key stakeholders understand what they need to do to change constraints, remove barriers, or add resources. Then publish the changes to your project plan so that all stakeholders will understand what is changing and how the team plans to accommodate the change.

Using this process, your project will be more fluid, but still under control. Your project will continue on its way with a plan that takes into account the shifting sands and changing needs of the real world.

Any project problem can be solved, but as a developer once said, "Scope, resources, timeline—you can change any two you want, but I get to change the third." In other words there are three key project constraints (scope, resources, time) and you can adapt as long as you can "stretch" one of the three when the other two change.

**Ask for estimates from the experts: those who will do the work.**

One of the key success factors of project planning is to have reliable estimates. Most project managers will tell you that project estimates are notoriously inaccurate, and that this is doubly true of IT projects. They claim that even when IT professionals add 50 to 100% as a "fudge factor," they still under-deliver function on late timelines because they run out of money. The usual approach is to blame this on the original estimates being faulty, but our experience does not support this claim. The problem is not the estimates, but that those estimates were made by the wrong people.

Experts provide the only reliable estimates. For reliable estimates of the time needed to do a development test, ask the developer. For a reliable estimate of what a product should cost, ask Procurement.

There is one caveat, however: while your experts provide the most reliable estimates, they will not be reliable estimators of their own availability because they usually are not assigning or prioritizing their own work. For example, a developer may estimate a task takes 40 hours to program, but that developer may only have 10 hours a week available to work on that task. In this situation the task will take four weeks, not one. This is why many people find they must double or triple development estimates.

While we are not fans of inflating estimates as a rule of thumb, we believe the exception to this rule is when your project management software tool assumes a forty hour work week. You need to take into account the actual availability of your resources. Even a "dedicated" resource will not be available to you forty hours a week because of administrative tasks—staff meetings, fire drills, emergencies, responding to emails, tying up loose ends on other projects. In this case it may be easier to use a multiplier on estimates to adjust the timeline accordingly.

**The project isn't over until it has fully rolled out and "settled in"**

After a project successfully produces its deliverables, there is a celebratory party. Then the team disbands and the problems begin. Two months past go-live: bugs are cropping up, sponsors are unhappy, and most of the organization has reverted to the old system, which it appears you can never shut down. There are no developers tasked with fixing the bugs, nor are there trainers available to help new users get past their learning curve. The real problem is that as a project
manager you did not realize that the project did not end at go-live.

Fortunately, you can easily prevent this scenario as long as the project plan takes into account that "project completion" really occurs weeks or months after the go-live date. There are always adjustments, "fixes" and other changes after implementation. The project deliverables (systems, new ways of working etc.) must be integrated into daily routines and business processes. Always secure post-launch funding in the budget, and keep a few team members available to accommodate these predictable and necessary adjustments. True success for a project includes its reputation six months to a year after it completes. Are people saying how great the "new" system, program, process, etc. is? Or are they saying this new system has made their job painful? You won't know if you are going to be successful immediately after the go-live date. It may take weeks or months to be certain of success.

There is one other post-launch closeout activity that is often neglected: documentation of lessons learned and best practices. A session to document lessons learned should be part of every project. In addition to documenting best practices, be sure to document actual-vs.-expected results, as well as other critical information required to measure the success of this project and help future projects adopt your best practices while avoiding pitfalls. Then publish this information (in Sharepoint, Wikis) where other project managers can easily find it.

## Conclusion: What Happened

*In the example that begins this chapter, the software project offered the potential for an enormous return on investment—if we could pull it off.*

*Previous projects had tried and failed, often because of the same hurdles that we faced. Finance would fund only a portion of the project, thus making the ROI more of a challenge. Legal would restrict how the system could be used. IT Operations would deny the request to support the application. Sometimes all three.*

*So how did we succeed? Simple: we involved the stakeholders at the beginning of the project.*

*Finance was a critical player early on. Our finance contact bought into the promise of the project and helped us craft the return-on-investment numbers. Then our finance contact ensured that our project was fully funded, since the bottom-line impact required doing all of it. One down, two to go.*

*Legal worked with us early in the project to define a set of parameters under which we would operate, including requiring us to approve each access request individually, to train each user in person, and to monitor the access regularly. Since Finance was already on board, funding the training was not a problem. And in retrospect—and perhaps ironically—Legal's restrictions turned out to be one of the key factors that ensured our success.*

*We suspected that IT Operations would be our biggest hurdle. Therefore, we ran our proof-of-concept out of their own product-evaluation laboratory. While we were working on our deliverables, parts of IT were figuring out how they were going to support these new tech-nologies. IT even offered suggestions on how to optimize these technologies, making our application better. When we got to the operations review meetings, everyone conceded that our exceptions were required because no other technologies could deliver what we had. Furthermore, IT already had proof that the technology worked, and they had a plan for supporting the application. Request approved.*

*The time it took to engage these groups was much less than the time that would have been spent working around their decisions. The product was better. We delivered it faster. And on a personal note, our reputations soared because we were the heroes who got Finance, HR, and IT Operations to say "yes." We became the experts on how to work with these groups.*

*The rest of the organization caught on quickly, and today its best practices include identifying and engaging all stakeholders as early as possible!*

**Key Lessons**

Focus on these key components of the Project Plan:

- Identifying and engaging stakeholders.
- Managing interdependencies among scope, resources and timeline.
- Estimating effectively.
- Rolling out the project.

Do not take the "do nothing" approach to scope creep, resource changes and time pressures.

Embrace the reality of having to meet altered stakeholder and sponsor expectations and ever-changing business needs—even if that means you have to re-plan the project.

The Project Plan should extend well beyond (weeks, possibly months) the "go live" point to stabilize the new system, processes, or business model, and to establish it as an accepted part of the organization.

## Chapter 2: Credibility and Influencing

*As a young Systems Engineer (SE) at IBM, I would hang out with the experienced SEs and listen to their war stories.*

*They discussed systems implementations that went smoothly from a technical perspective, but failed to result in the customers using the system productively and attaining the promised return on investment (ROI.) The employees who were supposed to use the system would circumvent it, put incorrect information in it—even on occasion sabotage the system—in order to make it appear that the correctly functioning computer was failing to perform.*

*The experienced SEs would shake their heads and say, "Well, I guess the dog won't eat the dog food."*

*Naively I asked what that meant. They told me the story of a dog food company that developed a highly nutritious new dog food with superior ingredients, only to discover that no one had thought to find out whether dogs enjoyed eating it.*

**Chapter Summary**

This chapter is for those who have helped lead a project before, but who are now "the one in charge," especially if they are leading a project for people with whom they have never worked.

The chapter explains how to establish credibility quickly in order to leverage it to influence the behavior of team members, sponsors and stakeholders.

Key concepts include always doing what you say you will do, coming to work with a positive outlook and using body language to set stakeholders at ease.

Have you ever finished a project and thought, "I've done all this work, now why don't they *love* me?!" Do you find yourself at the end of what seems to be a successful project, only to learn that you must have been on the wrong track all along because the people who are supposed to use the "new thing" (system, application, process, business model, behavior etc.) are balking? Or that those stakeholders who were supposed to help you were not quite as engaged as you were led to believe?

You must establish credibility and get buy-in and involvement from the stakeholders at the beginning of any project in order to prevent these failures. Don't run one of those "the dog won't eat the dog food" projects.

When new project managers ask, "what is the first step in a project?" experienced PMs correctly answer, "Getting a clear charter, followed by defining the scope and objectives of the project."

While technically that is the correct answer, in fact, there is a "before the first step" activity that needs to take place: establishing your credibility as the project manager.

**What is credibility?**

Like it or not, as a project manager you are in a position of leadership. You need the project team (also the sponsors, stakeholders and other project constituents) to follow you and do what you ask of them. Of course, generally the project manager, whether an internal employee or an external consultant, has no organizational authority over the team members. In other words, the project manager is not the person giving performance evaluations to the team members or sponsors at the end of the year. The project manager can *ask* for work from team members or resources from sponsors, but at the end of the day the person being asked can choose to ignore the request without much fear of consequences. *Only credibility stands between the project manager and abject failure.* People on the project must *want* the project, and the project manager, to succeed.

Credibility allows you to ask your team members for favors and give them tasks without having to prove to them that what you are asking is the right thing, or even their responsibility. They trust you. Your credibility causes people to willingly make a leap of faith simply because you have asked them to do so.

**Who is trustworthy?**

At this point many project managers may be questioning why they chose project management as a career. "Really? Credibility is going to make or break my ability to manage a project?" Yes.

The good news is that everyone else is pretty much like you—they trust and mistrust for the same reasons you do! So you will be able to figure out how you need to behave (and be) to *earn* the trust of your project team, manager, sponsors and other stakeholders, including vendors and external customers.

Let's play a game to figure out who is trustworthy, a "Trust Exercise." List three people whom you would trust to make life or death decisions for you, and why you trust them. Then list three people that you do *not* trust and why. (This list may also include things such as cars, computers, or institutions, in addition to people.)

The results of this exercise are surprisingly consistent. People tend to trust family members (parents, siblings, spouses, children), close friends whom they have known for many years, and religious or spiritual advisors (priests, nuns, rabbis, ministers, imams, monks etc.). Occasionally there is a long-time work colleague, manager, or executive who lands in the trust circle, but this is rare. As for people and institutions who are *not* trusted in America, politicians, public servants and government agencies lead the list, with used car salesmen and salespeople of all kinds following closely behind.

Continuing the debrief we find that the reasons to trust are usually something along the lines of "this person has always kept promises, helped me and told me the truth." The reasons not to trust are that people or institutions have "lied to" or misled the person, or have taken credit for work that person has done (e.g., a manager taking credit for a subordinate's work).

People also tend to mistrust "flavor of the month" organizational initiatives. When a project is perceived this way, the project manager has an uphill battle. People frequently think the new project (for example an ERP replacement) might go away if they ignore or resist it long enough. After all, many other projects have come and gone without imposing much lasting change.

There is also consistency in describing how a trusted leader (whether executive, manager, or project manager) makes one feel. According to Kouzes and Posner in their book, *Credibility* (p 30), people "working for leaders they admired" felt motivated, enthusiastic, capable, and supported; "no one mentioned fearful or intimidated or stupid or sad." So what characteristics do followers look for in a "credible leader?" We asked this question of numerous leadership program participants and their responses consistently included these descriptors:

- Approachable
- Reliable
- Confident
- Sympathetic
- Truthful
- Knowledgeable
- Respectful
- Good communicator
- Ethical

If these are words your project team, stakeholders, and clients use to describe you, you have a great start on establishing your credibility.

Establishing Credibility Quickly (before everything crashes down on your head)

Project managers, whether internal practitioners or external consultants, must quickly establish trust with their constituents to get their projects moving. Completing a task as straight-forward as defining scope and objectives can take an eternity if the stakeholders mistrust one another and/or you.

Project managers need credibility to gain the buy-in and engagement of their project team, sponsors, and stakeholders. How do you get that if you lack a multi-year track record with these people and are not a close relative or spiritual advisor to them (per our previous discussion of what makes people credible)? How do we acquire those universal trust-builders? Fortunately there are some simple ways to *earn* credibility:

- Set accurate expectations—then deliver (or over-deliver) on all promises

- Be candid, open, transparent (DWYSYWD—do what you say you will do)

- Develop and communicate shared goals and values

- Be willing to admit fault, errors and imperfection

- Be there for others; sustain a positive outlook

- Set expectations and deliver on them

If you know a project will take six months, do not agree to a three month timeline. You *must* insist on accurate plans. You can agree to something that is achievable in a best-case scenario as long as it includes contingency plans that take into account less-than-perfect conditions.

Delivering on promises and expectations is the simplest way to establish credibility. Start small. For example, promise a high-level, written project plan in two weeks, then deliver it in a week and a half. Make several small promises like this in the first few weeks of the project and deliver on them. Always "do what you say you will do" (DWYSYWD). People will begin to relax and trust you.

## Be candid, open, and transparent

It is better to tell ugly truths sooner rather than later. People will trust you if you are honest with them; they will mistrust you forever if they find out "the truth" from the rumor mill.

*As an example, an engagement that began as a data center consolidation (reducing six data centers to two locations) ultimately became an outsourcing engagement. The ROI simply was not there for consolidating. The executive sponsors were inclined not to tell the affected IT infrastructure leaders and staff until the last possible moment. But that would have meant many months of deception. If the affected staff were kept in the dark, we knew they would be suspicious, uncooperative and focused on resume-writing "just in case."*

*Fortunately, we got permission to share the high-level plan with the entire organization in a "town hall" meeting. The plan included requiring the outsourcer to hire at least 90% of the existing staff at comparable salaries and benefits. Being transparent paid off: during the 10-month engagement we had attrition of only one or two people out of an infrastructure staff of 300.*

## Develop and communicate shared goals and values

In any project with more than one team member, there will inevitably be conflict. The first step in conflict resolution, whether between two project team members or between stakeholders and the project team, is to find common goals between the conflicted parties. For instance, in most labor/management conflicts, keeping the company in business, and consequently keeping employees gainfully employed, tends to be a common goal of both labor and management.

For project managers there is one easy shared goal to establish: successful completion of the project and implementation of the new system, program, or process. You (the project manager) can be successful only if the project is successful. Since the success of a project is determined in great part by the satisfaction level of its sponsors and stakeholders, your goal of making your clients happy with the project's outcome is in perfect alignment with their own goal of wanting to *have* an outcome with which they are happy.

If you can persuade the sponsors, project team, and stakeholders that *their* success is how you define your own success, your credibility goes up by orders of magnitude. They will trust you not to lead them down the wrong path if they know your success is directly tied to theirs.

**Admit imperfection**

This is a fine line to walk. While you must be positive and confident to lead others successfully, you must also be willing to admit when you made a poor decision, got the facts wrong, or failed to accomplish something in the plan. For example, if you thought stakeholders would not need a second round of training right before go-live, and now you find they are making numerous errors that training could fix, admit you were mistaken and schedule some training.

Let people know you are human and fallible, just as they are. And let them know that you will forgive yourself, and them, for honest mistakes. You want them to tell you sooner rather than later when something has gone wrong or when they have made a bad decision or assumption. The best way to get them to trust you on this is to lead by example. Tell them you have made lots of mistakes in the past, but you have learned from them and will help them not to make the same mistakes.

## Be there

At some point (or points) during the project your team, stakeholders and even sponsors will have second thoughts, get discouraged, and have visions of "the project that ruined my career." A good project manager has to be equal parts confidant, career advisor, psychiatrist, and cheerleader. You don't have to *solve* people's problems. You do need to be a good listener, keep their confidential information completely to yourself, and encourage them when they have no hope.

Most importantly, you need to empathize. Notice we say "empathize" rather than "sympathize." Your team and sponsors do not need someone to feel sorry for them (*sympathize*); they need someone to understand what they are going through, their thoughts, emotions, fears and worries (*empathize*). They need to know that you understand them, to be reassured that their concerns are "normal," and, most of all, to know that you *care* about them. A colleague used to say, "They don't care how much you know until they know how much you care." This was his fundamental advice for new managers: *care about your people*. That goes double for project managers.

## Sustain a positive outlook

If you were on a project team where the project manager came in to work every day sluggish, depressed, moving slowly, and moaning about how terrible this project is and how its odds of success are non-existent, would you be motivated to do *your* best work? Or would you ask to transfer to a different project as soon as possible?

Whether you have an "upbeat" personality or not, as a project manager you *must* come to work with a positive, can-do attitude every day. Your energy level should boost others and inspire them to new levels of achievement. You need to be smiling and optimistic, even when things are not going well.

You should never ask of your team what you are not willing to do. If they need to come in early and stay late, you should keep the same (or longer) hours. Mutual sacrifices (like long hours) can be both a bonding opportunity and a credibility builder. Your actions are saying, "We're all in the same boat. Our joint efforts will sustain all of us." We have known project managers who never left the building before their last team member left. Yet also remember that exhausted people, even very smart ones, make mistakes. Insist that people take adequate amounts of time off and get enough sleep. Short bursts of fourteen-hour days can work, but sustained weeks, months, and years of overly long days will lead to disaster.

*By way of example, one of the authors learned the hard way what can happen when a programmer does not get enough sleep. While working on a data center move, we had a tech person working on a database that was not functioning correctly. Midnight was approaching, so we told him to pack up, go to the hotel, get some sleep, and start fresh in the morning. He said he would leave as soon as he finished one more thing. So we packed up and left. Returning the next morning, imagine our surprise to find that—five hours after he was told to get some sleep—the programmer made a catastrophic mistake and deleted a production database. As it turned out, the problem was compounded because the weekly and daily backups by the outsourcer had not run successfully for several weeks. Oops. So about three weeks of data had to be re-keyed by angry sales staff because an overtired tech person had made an error no one who was rested could possibly have made.*

*Don't just tell people to quit and go home—stand there until they actually do it. Their intentions are good, but inexperienced team members do not realize the potential for disaster they create by working when they are overly tired.*

## Influencing

Now that you have credibility, how do you use it to leverage influence? In other words how can credibility enable you to get the buy-in of stakeholders and *carte blanche* access to resources?

There are several theories surrounding the psychology of influencing.

## Social Learning Theory

Canadian-born Stanford University professor of psychology Albert Bandura proposed the modern Social Learning Theory. Bandura's Social Learning Theory states that people learn from one another through observation, imitation, and modeling.

So to "influence" someone's behavior you would "model" (demonstrate) the behavior you want them to exhibit. If they trust that you are more knowledgeable about the skill you are modeling than they are (i.e. you have credibility), they will imitate your behavior. In daily life we call this alternately "on the job training" or "professional development" (copying business behaviors of a more experienced worker).

## Personal or Vicarious Experience

What else influences people? According to Grenny et al in their book *Influencer*, "The greatest persuader is personal experience. The next best persuader is vicarious experience."

If you want someone to adopt something new (a software package, process, business model, or behavior), the best way is to give them personal experience with the "new" thing. In other words, let them take a test drive of the software or process and see for themselves how much more quickly and easily they can do their job. Or show them new tasks they can do that would not be possible with the old system, process, or model.

Providing vicarious experience through artful storytelling can also help you influence your project team and stakeholders. The use of "war stories" can be both educational and influential. Your people do not have to experience a catastrophic event to learn how to respond to one—they just have to hear a story of an event you went through and what you would do the same way, or differently, if it happened again. A disaster is much better experienced vicariously than in real life.

## Body Language

Another aspect of influencing is body language. You need to be sure your body is saying the same thing your mouth is. To build trust and influence others, start with a smile. Smiling says the same thing in all languages: "I like you; I want to be friends." Of course there are sincere smiles and fake smiles. Sincere smiles are quick; they start small, then crest, then disappear. Fake smiles are plastered on your face. You know the difference; so does everyone you meet.

Another helpful body language tool is "mirroring." When your body position looks similar to that of the person with whom you are talking, it sets them at ease. If they lean forward, so do you. If they cross their legs, so do you. Dressing similarly to your clients (stakeholders, project team members, sponsors) also sets them at ease.

Basically, people like people who are like themselves. The more they find in common with another person (from their physical appearance to where they went to school to where they have lived), the easier they find it to like that person.

So be sure to dress appropriately, use body language (smile, mirror), and quickly find the life milestones you have in common with your stakeholders (hometown, schools, kids, hobbies, music, books, travel, etc.). Salespeople are generally taught how to set their clients at ease. Project managers—and frankly all business professionals—should also learn the rudimentary psychology behind relationship building. Establishing a solid working relationship with anyone always begins by getting acquainted and finding reasons to like one another. Make that process easy for your clients, sponsors and stakeholders.

## Listening

As the old saw goes, "You have two ears and one mouth; you should listen twice as much as you talk." Listening is a lost art. Most people are polite enough to wait for their turn to talk, but few are actually listening to the person speaking. When listening, it is important to observe and interpret body language and tone of voice to get the full meaning of the speaker's message. Is this person nervous, stressed, fearful, acting as though (s)he knows something (s)he is not telling? A message is so much more than the words.

Once you have listened, process what you have heard—both the words and the emotional state of the speaker. Then ask questions; confirm what you heard and clarify any unclear aspects. Once you feel you have all the relevant information, you can begin composing a response. Do you need to reassure this person? Explain more details about what will happen at the end of the project? You may need to identify the resources to be used on the project so this person understands (s)he is not on the hook to provide staff. What is the concern, whether clearly expressed or hidden, in the message and what does this person *need* from you?

## Summary

The key thing to understand about influencing is that it cannot begin until you have credibility with those you are attempting to influence. Be sure to model the behaviors you need from your team, sponsors and stakeholders. Give stakeholders both personal and vicarious experience with whatever is new. Defusing fear of the unknown through hands-on experience is often a key factor in quelling resistance to change as well as influencing behavior. And finally, listen. Be sure you understand what people object to, what they need from you and what their expectations are.

## Key Lessons

## Credibility

Establish expectations accurately, communicate continuously and make *sure* you listen carefully to (and act on) all feedback.

Deliver on promises, and when possible, over-deliver. Always do what you say you will do. (DWYSYWD)

Shifting Sands

Accept that you are imperfect and so is everyone else; be forgiving, learn from mistakes—both your own and others'.

Come to work every day with a positive outlook. Mountains *can* be moved, one shovelful at a time.

**Influencing**

Influence by modeling behaviors; project team members take their cue from your actions.

Use body language to improve relationships and set clients/colleagues at ease.

Remember that listening is almost always a more important skill than talking.

Use personal stories and provide hands-on experiences to influence decisions.

Exercise (or at least explore) all six "levers of influence" described in the book *Influencer*.

Jana Markowitz and William Berghel

# Chapter 3: Organizational Change Management and Communications

"Nothing is permanent, but change."

—*Heraclitus, 535–475 BCE, philosopher*

*We started an IT infrastructure project for a client, but after that was successfully underway, they asked us to take over another project that was "stuck." So I stepped in to replace two full-time contract project managers on an enterprise software implementation project that had been underway for a year and a half and "in parallel" with the old system for six months, with no end in sight.*

*After many weeks of poking, prodding and turning over stones, I figured out that everything was working as promised in the new system. Only one thing had been forgotten: the most powerful people in the organization had used the old, green-screen system for twenty years. They knew the old system, knew the short cuts and trusted its results (although it was a custom application with no documentation indicating how any of the financial numbers were calculated!).*

*No one had asked these powerful users if they were ready to switch to the new system and they were certain they were not ready. Hence the abrupt halt of the project.*

**Chapter Summary**

Everyone needs to read this chapter, even if you are not planning to run a project. Change happens with or without projects and understanding how to make it flow forward correctly is critical. Clear, timely communications are also crucial to organizations. Unfortunately, we have found communications in most organizations are done poorly, too late or not at all.

Key concepts include common reactions to change, the roles in change management, elements of a change plan and the four goals of communication.

## The Nature of Change

Everything that is new and shiny one day becomes old and worn out—clothes, cars, appliances—and yes, even business systems, business processes, and business models. Technology is often either a catalyst or an enabler of change. This means that when someone says, "We need a new system," what they probably mean is that they need a new process or business model, and installing a new system almost always requires a re-think or re-design of the business processes. Thus it is not really technology that forces people to change. Instead, an executive decides a change is necessary, and selects technology to facilitate that change, forcing employees to learn new procedures, software and ways of navigating their work.

## Common Reactions to Change

Resistance to change is normal and pervasive. If you are running a project, which by definition means you are changing *something*, you will undoubtedly encounter resistance.

Over time we have identified four fundamental reasons for resistance to change (or resistance to *being changed*):

- Perception of loss
- Misunderstanding or lack of trust
- Different assessment of the situation or needs
- Lack of self-confidence or fear

When you are removing a system which stakeholders have used (and cursed at) for many years, they actually perceive loss—loss of the system they know how to manipulate and circumvent. Now they have to learn new ways to be devious. Some change can even trigger a response that looks like the five stages of grief. (See Notes at the end of this chapter for the five stages of grief and how to recognize them.)

Lack of trust frequently crops up when you implement a new system. How do they know you aren't palming something off on them that won't even perform as well as their current "piece-of-garbage" system? After all, you (or someone in IT) picked the current system and it's *awful*, so your judgment must be questionable. Their lack of trust in your judgment (and the judgment of the corporate execs) is almost a certainty. That is why they will be pushing back against and undermining your project.

Or perhaps they understand what you want to do (put in that new system)—they may even have participated in a needs assessment—but they think there is a better solution. The better idea is their own, of course. And they think your system will not solve all the problems *their* solution would solve. Their assessment of what is needed to fix "the problem" differs from yours.

Or they spent twenty years learning the ins-and-outs of the current system. Now you want to put in something new, and they are not sure they are up to the task of learning this new thing. It looks *nothing like* the current system—and those new employees are going to learn it quickly and perhaps make the more seasoned workers look less knowledgeable than they do on the old system, where they are very skilled. Commonly heard: "Grumble, grumble, why can't you just leave things alone until I retire?"

People do not resist new ideas or new systems; they resist giving up comfortable, habitual behaviors. Try this Change Exercise to demonstrate to yourself how a very insignificant change can cause discomfort.

1. Cross your arms. Not take note of which hand is "on top" of your arm.

2. Now cross your arms with the *opposite* hands over and under as you did originally.

Most people find this exercise difficult to do and uncomfortable. Now imagine being told you must *always* cross your arms this new way in the future. Apply this new understanding of how change "feels" to the project environment. Just think about the way people must feel when you tell them *every familiar task they do at work every day* must change with the new system. What you may view as a minor change in the work process could be a life-changing and traumatic event in the perception of the people having to make the change part of their daily lives.

**Common Change Management Frameworks**

So how do you "plan change" in a way that minimizes resistance and maximizes project productivity? There are several popular change management frameworks, all based on the same organizational behavior research done over the last forty years. While people versed in each methodology swear that their method is the *only* way to be successful, the truth is they all work. Variances in outcome are more likely to be related to the project manager's and sponsor's ability to communicate, negotiate and manage relationships than to the change methodology used.

There are several change-management frameworks—from ProSci's ADKAR (Awareness, Desire, Knowledge, Ability, Reinforcement) method to William Bridges' three stage model in *Managing Transitions* (see Appendix). For the novice, we recommend following John Kotter's 8 Step Model:

1. Create a sense of urgency
2. Form a guiding coalition (sponsors)
3. Create a vision
4. Communicate the vision
5. Empower others to act on the vision
6. Create quick wins
7. Build on the change

8. Institutionalize the change

Whether you rigidly follow one method or create your own, the key is to plan and manage the transition in a structured manner. All methods acknowledge the old ways or systems before moving to the new ways. All methods recognize that people prefer small changes to big ones, but that sometimes a clean break is better than death-by-a-thousand-cuts.

**Roles in Change Management**

Regardless of the methodology used, there are three roles in any change initiative:

- Sponsor
- Change Agent
- Change Target

Sponsors are the executives who have a business reason to want change. They procure resources, use their personal brand and political clout to promote the project and remove barriers when possible. Sponsors are the people to whom project managers report on project status.

Change Agents include project managers, project management offices (PMOs), project team members and consultants. Their role is to plan, implement, and report on the change.

Change Targets are the managers, individual contributors, customers, and suppliers whose role is to adapt to the change and continue performing their business function in the new environment.

Some people may be both Change Agents and Change Targets. For example, project managers are *always* Change Agents. If they are employees of the organization undergoing change, they may also be Change Targets. (Almost never is the project manager a Sponsor, although it is theoretically possible.)

**Elements of a Change Plan**

Any Change Plan has at minimum four key elements:

- Stakeholder Analysis
- Metrics
- Communication Plan
- Training Plan

Stakeholder Analysis is the identification of all people—both inside and outside of the organization—who are impacted by the change. It assesses:

- Degree of commitment of each stakeholder (for, neutral, against)
- Their level of influence (high, medium, low)
- The degree to which they are impacted (high, medium, low)
- Their perception of project impact—Loss/Threat, Benefit /Gain
- Level of commitment desired from this stakeholder
- Key Actions to gain the stakeholders' commitment
- Key Messages about the project purpose and timeline to gain buy-in

Metrics are the way we take a project's temperature. How do we know when we are done? How do we know whether the project is on schedule and whether quality standards are being met? How do we know if the change efforts have been effective? For that matter, how do we judge whether the change itself has accomplished its planned goal? Metrics should also monitor and evaluate the effectiveness of communications and training. Do we need more of either? Defining and tracking the right metrics for a project is a critical success factor. We will discuss metrics further in Chapter 6.

The Communications Plan must define to whom we communicate, what the key messages are, what medium we use (teleconference, in person meeting, town hall, videoconference, webinar, social media) who delivers the message, when and how often to communicate.

The Training Plan defines how the project intends to educate people on how to do their current jobs in the new environment. Some projects require initial training, a booster session just before cutover, post-implementation training, and advanced or "Super-User" training. You may want to video the basic introductory training so it can be reused for orientation and training of new employees. You should get feedback on and make adjustments to training just as you do with communications.

Note that these topic-specific plans must be integrated with the overall project plan and must be adjusted and adapted as the project plan changes.

**Critical Success Factors for a Change Plan**

It is critically important to get a small handful of people-issues right. Based on our experience there are five critical success factors for a change plan.

Change Targets must trust and believe the Change Sponsor(s) and Change Agents. Without trust in place the Change Targets will blatantly ignore rules, requests, deadlines, and other things that can destroy your project before it gets off the ground. Building trust and credibility *has* to be any project manager's first step.

Stakeholder expectations must be accurately set. Whether the PMO, the project manager, consultants, or the sponsor sets those expectations, they must be realistic and accurate. You cannot tell someone the project will be done in three months and expect to have any credibility when you are only halfway through six months later. Make accurate estimates, add a fudge factor and work your and the team's fannies off trying to make your deadlines.

People should be given information before they discover it on their own. When people "discover" a truth before you tell them the truth, you lose everything—trust, credibility, integrity. No one will follow you if they think you have "lied by omission." Secrets are very poorly kept in large corporations, so do not count on keeping them for very long. Find a way to make basic information available and easily accessible. Transparency makes everyone's life easier.

Adequate training must be provided. Training is the key to making people comfortable doing their work in the new environment. Whether this training is from a vendor, is custom-created internally, or is some blend of the two depends on the specific situation. Figure out how this is going to work, who has to do what, and how this will be funded. Your overarching project plan should include every possible type of training that will be required—even if it is not something the corporate entity is funding or providing.

No one should have more change forced upon them than they can accommodate. Before you agree to be the project manager of an initiative, take a step back and assess the organization's capacity for change. Have you just completed a major merger or acquisition? Have you had seven change initiatives launched in the last six months? How agile, adaptable, and resilient are the people and departments who will be part of the project? Be sure your people and organization have the capacity to absorb more change before you pour it on—otherwise it may just roll off them like water off a duck's back, as we say in the South.

## Communications

"The single biggest problem in communication is the illusion that it has taken place."

—*George Bernard Shaw, 1856–1950, English author*

## Goals of Communication

There are four goals (which are also stages) of communication:

- Awareness
- Engagement
- Commitment
- Action

While these stages are sequential, different parts of the organization and even certain individuals may be at different stages. You want to make people cognizant of the coming change (Awareness), then get them to understand and agree that the change is needed (Engagement), secure their buy-in to the plan (Commitment), and set them in motion to implement the change (Action).

Note that people can slip back from one stage to a previous one especially if they hit opposition or discover problems or barriers.

## Who needs to be aware of this change?

Everyone—even those who don't appear to be impacted—needs to understand what is happening, who will be involved, and what the expected outcome is. They need to know because even if their area is not changing, change in other parts of the organization can have a 'ripple effect' on everyone. Understanding what is *not* changing can provide comfort and reassurance, especially to those who must endure the most intense change.

## What's in it for me?

People who are engaged care about the project, understand why it's important to the company, and want it to succeed.

If the people who are supposed to perform the tasks in the project plan are *not* engaged, you will find that your project is at the bottom of their To-Do list—or possibly not on their list at all.

If you cannot persuade team members that their effort and actions are required, that the change is required, that the organization and their job will not survive without the change, then your project will not be on-time, on-budget or successful. There must always be a "burning platform"—a compelling reason that motivates the stakeholder to "jump" from their current, comfortable, familiar state into the unknown.

Engagement is *crucial*.

**What is commitment?**

Sometimes commitment is a leap of faith. The change initiative must have the dedication and determination of people at all levels—executive, middle management, and individual contributor.

Commitment means that when you hit a brick wall, you get up immediately and start figuring out if you are going over, under, or around it; or if none of those options work, you figure out which twenty friends can help you tear down the wall.

Commitment can only come from workers who are willing to give you "above and beyond" effort. Showing up for eight hours each day is *not* commitment.

Commitment, or lack of it, determines behavior after cutover, as well. In a help desk call after a cutover, the non-committed worker will say, "Here is what's wrong with *your* system. How soon will you have it fixed?" The committed worker will say, "I've found a problem in the system—what can I do to help you fix this? And, by the way, I have already figured out a workaround which you can share with others." The former wants the system to fail; the latter wants it to succeed.

**Action**

Once project roles and responsibilities are clear, everyone involved in the project must execute. Project managers and the PMO should keep all levels informed of status, issues and resource/skill needs. They should also remove barriers.

During the Action stage make sure everyone knows what problems exist, who is working on them and when they are expected to be resolved. There are so many interdependencies in most projects that a problem which seems small may bring the whole project to a standstill if the project manager does not know of the need to re-schedule tasks to work around the issue.

Of course in all stages of communication listening to messages is as important as sending messages. Project managers frequently get busy and only half-listen to team members. Be sure to maintain focus and listen carefully. Any daily communication could contain mission-critical information.

**Integrating the Change Plan into the Project Plan is Crucial**

Of course all four of the Change Plan's sub-plans—Stakeholder Analysis, Metrics, Communication Plan and Training Plan—are things which can be created and tracked separately from the overall project plan. But why would you? For example, if key project plan dates change, will the training be delivered at the right time? It won't if the Training Plan was not integrated into the main project plan.

While combinations of consultants and internal staff members may be in charge of various parts of the project, and the organizational change management piece may be in the hands of special consultants, you must *never* let them maintain their plan completely outside of the overall project plan. Confidential details might be kept separately to protect proprietary information or methodologies, but the placeholder task for completion of a specific chunk of work must be included in the overall project plan. You have to be able to track and know whether this chunk of work is on-time, and whether it is still positioned in the right time and order relative to other tasks.

**Key Lessons**

Your project will not die because of technical issues, no matter how dire they may seem. Your project *will* die because of the way you respond to issues, whether they are technical, political or interpersonal.

Resilience, adaptability and problem-solving are essential competencies for a project manager.

The 3 Roles in Change are: Sponsor, Change Target, Change Agent

A Change Plan includes at minimum:

- Stakeholder Analysis
- Metrics
- Communication Plan
- Training Plan

The Stages/Goals of Communication are:

- Awareness
- Engagement,
- Commitment
- Action

The Five Stages of Grief (Denial, Anger, Bargaining, Depression and Acceptance), are often seen as a reaction to change.

Common Change Frameworks include ProSci's ADKAR, Bridges' Stages of Transition, and Kotter's 8 Steps

**Notes**

Types of Organizational Change

There are at least three types of organizational change:

- Transitional change (the kind that accompanies projects, reorganizations and mergers / acquisitions)

- Continuous improvement change (for example Six Sigma)

- Transformational change (when an entire culture, mindset or industry is irrevocably changed—think game changers like the introduction of the personal computer or, more recently, the iPhone and iPad)

For project management purposes we only discuss transitional change. However, while you are running projects, you may be asked to lead the other types of change as well. We will provide a substantial list of suggested reading at the end of the book, which can bring you up to speed enough to cope with this situation if it arises.

The Five Stages of Loss

Because change can have a dramatic effect on people, especially if it is thrown at them rapid-fire without adequate preparation, it is not too surprising that some people, or even whole departments or organizations, may react to change by going through the classic stages of loss/grief.

You may recognize the classic five stages of loss in a project when you hear the following kinds of comments:

**Denial**

"This is just flavor-of-the-month. If we hold out, they will come to their senses and ditch this project. Just ignore those emails asking you to prepare for change."

**Anger**

"This #$%^& project is wrecking my plans for sales growth. They are taking people I need to accomplish my business goals. I am going to the VP to let her know how this project is damaging the bottom line!"

**Bargaining**

"Just let me get through one more year and I'll retire. Then you can turn on this new system."

**Depression**

"I'm going to be demoted or fired. There's no way I can learn this fast enough to survive. This whole company is going to go out of business. There's no hope for us."

**Acceptance**

"Well, I hate the new system, but at least we are back to focusing on the customer. I guess it's no worse than that previous piece-of-garbage system."

Common Change Management Frameworks: ADKAR

ADKAR is a method created and taught by consulting firm ProSci. They produce change managers certified in the ADKAR methodology. Their method proposes using planning, training and coaching to achieve the outcomes represented by their acronym: Awareness, Desire to change, Knowledge, Ability and Reinforcement.

After a five-day certification class most business executives know enough about change that they realize they need to hire experienced change managers for their projects. ProSci is happy to point people to firms with teams of ADKAR-certified change managers.

## Common Change Management Frameworks: William Bridges' *Managing Transitions*

William Bridges details in his book *Managing Transitions* how to guide, coax, coach and manage people through change. His model for change has three stages:

1. Ending the old ways
2. Neutral – the time when people have "let go" of the old, but have not yet bought into, and grabbed onto, the new
3. Beginning the new—when people understand and embrace the new system, behaviors and goals

## Common Change Management Frameworks: John Kotter's Eight Step Model for Change Management

1. Create a sense of urgency
2. Form a guiding coalition (sponsors)
3. Create a Vision
4. Communicate the Vision
5. Empower others to act on the vision
6. Create quick wins
7. Build on the Change
8. Institutionalize the Change

# Chapter 4: Conflict Resolution, Issue Resolution and Coping with Resistance

"After an argument silence may mean acceptance or the continuation of resistance by another means."

—*Mason Cooley, 1927–2002, Professor of English, aphorist*

**Chapter Summary**

Once a person has managed one project, (s)he will understand the value of conflict resolution, issue tracking and strategies to address resistance. Everyone, new or experienced, project manager or not, will benefit from the skills taught in this chapter.

Key concepts include the five approaches to conflict resolution (according to the Thomas-Kilmann theory), the importance of having a decision process for issue resolution and the dos and don'ts of dealing with resistance to change.

**Understanding Conflict Resolution**

Conflict means different things to different people—from red-faced yelling matches to cordial, collegial debates. When discussing conflict related to project management, the simplest, broadest definition will probably serve us best. For our purposes a conflict is any situation in which two or more people's concerns, opinions or desired outcomes differ.

Conflict can be quiet, civil and minor, or it can be loud, offensive and violent. Which it is, or which it becomes, is entirely dependent on the choices made by those involved.

The key phrase to remember when dealing with conflict is, "pick your battles." In other words what is at stake in this conflict? Is it something so important that it is worth enduring confrontational behavior? Engendering bad feelings? Potentially creating life-long enemies? Are you certain this difference is *that* important?

## What causes conflict?

The most common causes of conflict during a project are workload, time pressure and stress. People are not at their best when they feel pressured, and a big project is essentially a pressure cooker.

When your project team becomes irritable, moody and over-reactive, it is probably because they are behind schedule, under-resourced and experiencing scope creep. Moreover, if the project is like this now, they dread to think how much worse it may get later. Team members come to work sleep-deprived, worried and stressed. No wonder there is conflict among project teams; the environment almost always becomes toxic, at least for a short time, even if you have the very best project manager and team members.

But conflict on a project can stem from more than just stress. Other sources of conflict include the following:

- Personality clashes
- Ideological differences (Linux vs Windows, Oracle vs SQL Server, etc)
- Different life experiences
- Different cultural norms, values, beliefs, perceptions or assumptions

In addition to conflict between individuals, which we describe above, there can also be conflict between departments and teams. This conflict is usually caused by one of the following differences:

- Short-term pressures and long-term goals differ— Shareholders may expect a quarterly profit at a time when the company really needs to make huge expenditures to fulfill long-term plans.

- Lack of clarity—Vaguely defined responsibilities may leave some tasks without any owner and other tasks with two groups fighting over who must perform them.

- Competition for limited resources—Two teams may argue about who gets a sole resource (perhaps a Crystal Reports programmer) when both need the resource immediately and for a long time.

- Personal needs including power, status, ego, recognition, self-worth—Sometimes specific people in an organization have to get their way just because it shows how powerful they are (no matter what it does to your project deliverables and timeline).

- Regional attitudes—If your virtual team consists of team members in New York, Alabama and China, then differences in culture, time zone and accents alone could doom your project.

- The pace of change—Some people do not want to let go of the old; others move too quickly forward.

Sometimes even the daily habits or behaviors of team members can cause friction. For example

- How team members ask for help—Do they act entitled and condescending, or appreciative of the help?

- How the team deals with problems—Do they panic, alarming others, or do they approach the problem calmly and analytically?

- How the team determines "fault"—Do they play the "blame game?" Or do they seek process flaws or root cause events instead of trying to find a scapegoat?

- Personal work styles—Are they structured in handling deadlines and prioritization of tasks? Or are they spontaneous and flexible?

- How members communicate with one another daily—Do they speak respectfully to each other, or are they abrupt, rude and dismissive?

Conflict between teams can be over things as trivial as workspace or as big as how rewards and recognition are distributed and whether metrics are applied to entire teams when only one individual can impact the outcome.

**Handling Conflict**

Notice the words "different" or "differing" occur frequently in the causes of conflict. If we see things differently, we tend to slide quickly into conflict. The good news is that conflict resolution does not *always* have to be confrontational with a "winner" and "loser" in the battle.

How we choose to resolve conflicts impacts relationships, stress levels, morale, effectiveness and productivity.

Relationships are often measured in years. How you resolve differences in the early stages of a work relationship can either establish a strong foundation of trust and mutual respect or can limit, for how-ever long the relationship endures, the level of support you give each other. You might win a battle and lose the war.

Behavioral scientists Dr. Kenneth Thomas and Dr. Ralph Kilmann developed a set of five conflict resolution "modes" (approaches). Their Thomas-Kilmann Instrument (TKI) is based on the '60s research of Blake and Mouton, and was published in the mid-70s, but was re-normed in 2007. The good news is that your "preferred" conflict resolution style (which is what the TKI measures) is not a limiting factor in your ability to resolve conflict. Everyone is capable of learning all five approaches and using them in the appropriate situations, so which one or two approaches come most naturally to you will not matter if you are consciously choosing the method to use in a specific situation.

## TKI's Five Conflict Handling Modes

Thomas and Kilmann's conflict resolution theory proposes that there are two basic aspects which determine the approach needed for a specific situation: cooperativeness and assertiveness. Assertiveness is the degree to which you attempt to satisfy your own concerns, while cooperativeness is the degree to which you try to satisfy the concerns of others[1]

The conflict mode you choose should be determined by your personal skill set (e.g., are you good at calming, mediating, negotiating?) and our assessment of the situation (e.g., is the other person likely to agree to a compromise?)

All five conflict resolution modes are effective if used appropriately. The Thomas-Kilmann approach takes into account the fact that each situation is unique and people must operate within their own skill sets.

We often rely on one or two modes out of habit. This may be because we are comfortable with our skills in this mode, because we have seen others resolve conflict this way, or because this approach has brought success to us in the past.

Thomas and Kilmann propose all conflict situations can be addressed by one of the following five conflict resolution approaches[2]:

- **Competing** (Confronting)—"My way or the highway." The goal of this approach is to arrange it so "we" win and "others" lose.

- **Collaborating**—"Two heads are better than one." The goal of this approach is to find a "win-win" solution.

---

[1] Kenneth W. Thomas, *Introduction to Conflict Management*, CPP, Inc., 2002.
[2] *Ibid.*

- **Compromising**—"Let's make a deal!" The goal of this approach is to find a "middle ground," a solution everyone can live with and support. But achieving a compromise means everyone must give up some part of their desired outcome.

- **Avoiding**—"I'll think about that tomorrow," the Scarlett O'Hara approach. The goal of this approach is to delay any resolution that might impact the relationship, but not to give in (accommodate) at least for the moment.

- **Accommodating**—"It would be my pleasure." The goal of this approach is to yield completely to the other person, giving up all of your desired outcomes.

## Time, Resources and Choosing a Conflict Resolution Mode

Let's look at each approach and determine when it should, and should not, be used.

## Confronting

Confronting is quicker than compromising or collaborating. The leader, or whoever is the most powerful person in the conflict, simply imposes his or her will.

In emergencies, such as life or death situations, you want a dictatorial-decision maker, who knows what he or she is doing, to take charge and tell people what to do.

In the majority of corporate environments however, Confronting should be a last resort because it can create enemies and inspire vindictiveness. Use Confronting sparingly, and give careful consideration to alternatives before doing so.

## Collaborating

Collaborating is defined as both sides working on an optimal solution rather than insisting on their own way. In collaboration both sides should get all of their desired outcomes, making it the approach with the fewest negative side effects.

Collaborating brings benefits in addition to resolving the problem; it builds collaborative work skills in the participants, improves communications between the parties and lets them see an alternative to "win-lose" scenarios. Collaborating also forces both sides to better understand the other's perspective. This method creates instant buy-in for the solution, since both parties helped develop it.

Use this method when both sides of the issue are important and interdependent.

There is, however, one downside to Collaborating: it is the most time-consuming and expensive resolution method.

**Compromising**

Compromising means finding a middle ground or foregoing some part of your concerns in order to have others' needs met. You may negotiate what to keep and what to give up, or you may "split the difference."

If an issue is important, but not critical, it isn't worth "battling" for (Confronting) or spending a lot of time and money on (Collaborating), so Compromising becomes the approach of choice.

Compromising keeps the power even and avoids damaging the relationship.

Sometimes the compromise stage is an interim solution until more time, or additional resources, can be applied to finding a collaborative solution.

Alternatively, if you have already tried Confronting and Collaborating, but still could not reach an agreement, Compromising may be the only approach left that actually resolves the problem at hand.

**Avoiding**

With the Avoiding approach no one's issues are resolved, which may be seen as stalling or ignoring the issue. But when an issue is trivial, resolving it does not matter. Especially if the issue is between two individuals, the project manager may prefer to let them resolve it and not intervene. (Pick your battles.)

There may also be tense times when it is better to overlook minor infractions rather than fight about them. (Again, pick your battles.) Or if you need more information, you may need to delay making a decision until you have time to reconnoiter.

If you are in a position of little power or control, it may be wise to stay out of unimportant issue resolution. (Pick your battles.)

If the problem at hand is a symptom, sometimes it is better to ignore it and go after the root cause instead.

All of these are reasons, or rationalizations, for avoiding the conflict, which can sometimes mean having to dodge people in the hallway or at meetings.

The appropriate time to use the Avoiding approach is when the relationship is more important than the issue.

## Accommodating

Accommodating involves setting aside your own wants and needs completely in deference to others. It may be an act of selfless generosity or simply obeying orders from above with which you may not agree completely. It could also be a sign of respect for the person or group with whom you are in conflict.

There are several good reasons to accommodate, including:

- Reasonableness—If you realize you may not be 100% right and relent, you are showing reasonableness.

- Developing performance—When you allow someone to do things their own way, they learn and grow; this encourages reasonable risk-taking and empowerment.

- Goodwill—Yielding to someone puts them in the position of "owing you one."

- Peace (remember pick your battles?)—Sometimes winning on a specific issue is just not worth the effort. It is especially desirable to preserve harmony and avoid discord in times of turmoil.

- Retreating—If you have already been overridden on a decision, there is no point in continuing to fight.

- Perspective—If the issue is more important to the other person than to you, it may be worthwhile for you to give in. That way they "owe you one."

On the following page is a helpful guide to the five methods of conflict resolution and their effects.

## METHODS FOR RESOLVING CONFLICTS—WHAT HAPPENS

| Method | What Happens | When to Use | When Not to Use |
|---|---|---|---|
| **Compete/Confront** "My way or the highway" | Position or strength is used to settle the disagreement | For issues of a legal or ethical nature; when authority is expected to decide | When this leaves "loser" powerless to express concerns |
| **Collaborate** "Two heads are better than one" | Mutual respect allows parties to work together to resolve issues | When time permits and parties work as "us vs problem" rather than "us vs them" | Time, money, commitment and ability are not available |
| **Compromise** "Let's make a deal!" | Each party gives up something to reach a compromise | Both parties are better off with a compromise rather than win/lose | When compromise is so far from both positions that no one is likely to commit |
| **Avoid** "I'll think about that tomorrow," as Scarlett O'Hara said. | People deny the existence of a problem or avoid being together | When preservation of a relationship is more important than the issue or decision | When avoiding the problem just gives it more time to fester |
| Accommodate "It would be my pleasure" | One party yields | To preserve a relationship | When the issue is vital or will negatively impact the organization |

**Source: International Federation of University Women, modified with TKI terms**

We highly recommend the booklet *Introduction to Conflict Management*, from CPP, which more fully explains the Thomas-Kilmann conflict resolution method. It is available at www.cpp.com. We also recommend online or instructor-led training on TKI conflict resolution.

**Issue Resolution**

In any project issues will arise. The key is to document them immediately and in great detail, determine what person, people or organization will be responsible for resolving them and the date by which they will be completed.

It is also critically important to identify all stakeholders who will be impacted by the issue and/or solution—even if these people are not "officially" responsible for choosing a resolution. Let's call these people "interested parties." If you leave interested parties out of the loop when developing a solution, you will find you have opponents and possibly massive resistance when you try to implement.

You can have an easy to use issue-tracking tool by simply creating a spreadsheet with headings reflecting the information above (Issue Description, Date Opened, Person/People Responsible, Date Due) plus a column for status—Open, Closed—and a Notes column. You can share this issue log with the entire team on Sharepoint, in a Wiki or via other collaborative technologies.

It is customary to review issues in project team meetings, discuss status and, when necessary, change ownership or add resources to move the resolution along.

This all sounds so simple. So why do project teams sometimes end up in knock-down, drag-out fights over minor issues?

Sometimes team members or groups have prior reasons for animosity ("history") and use any excuse, even minor project issues, to re-start their battle.

Sometimes an issue that seems minor to you is of very major concern to one person or group. And sometimes this person or group may not even be an identified stakeholder. Be sure to analyze those impacted by an issue carefully so you can include them in solving the problem.

Sometimes people who have been on a project a long time are tired, irritable and at the end of their rope. It does not take much to push them over the edge. Even a tiny issue that is unresolved can spark the explosion.

So track the issues, discuss them and meticulously document them. But use your facilitation skills to move people along if a meeting appears to be headed into battle mode over an issue.

Some facilitation techniques that have worked for us include calling a break at the strategic moment when things are about to explode. This gives people time to cool down and decide against violent acts or outbursts.

There is also the "Parking Lot" (a flip chart with "Parking Lot" at the top) where you can put discussions that are tangential to the main topic. Be sure to return to these topics at the end of the meeting. Some Parking Lot topics may become Logged Issues, while others may be addressed or deemed unimportant by the end of the meeting.

Or you could escalate the touchy issue by assigning it to a person who is higher in the organization than *both* of the people in conflict in your meeting. This tends to shut things down pretty quickly.

You should also have an agreed-to decision process to apply to issues. For example, on extremely large projects (ones involving multiple departments and dozens or even hundreds of team members), it is fairly common to create a "Decision Rights Matrix" (topics down the left, individuals or groups along the top) that shows for each issue/topic which individuals or departments have which kind of Decision-Making Authority—for example, Decision-Maker, Input-Provider, Expert, Receives FYI Updates. That way no one mistakenly thinks (s)he is "in charge" when in fact, someone else is making the final decision. Without a clear decision-making process, and clearly identified decision maker(s), you risk sparking major conflicts.

You will also need to identify a point at which analysis must end and a decision must be made. Otherwise you risk the situation known as "analysis paralysis." There is always going to be "one more look" that might yield a different (or more desirable) answer. But at some point you must "fish or cut bait" and choose a path. No choice is so final that you cannot come back to that intersection and try the other fork in the road. But there must be a decision made and action taken. Many projects wander off course and even die because of "analysis paralysis." Make the best choice you can with the information available and forge ahead.

Remember to carefully analyze who will be impacted by the solution and be sure to get their input on (or at minimum keep them informed about) the solutions under discussion. Blame and regret arrive when you are blindsided by an "interested party" who has the authority to derail your entire project if (s)he does not like your choice of solution for an issue.

**Causes of Resistance to Change**

Change frequently brings with it resistance, but why? Peter Senge, author of *The Fifth Discipline*, said, "People don't resist change. They resist being changed!" As mentioned in Chapter 3, we have identified four fundamental reasons for people to resist being changed:

- Perception of loss

- Misunderstanding or lack of trust

- Different assessment of the situation or needs

- Lack of self-confidence or fear

Understanding that these things spark resistance, what can you do to either prevent or cope with the resulting resistance?

**Coping with Resistance**

If you have been hearing negative chatter about your project in the hallways or the restrooms, you may want some pointers on how to prevent and/or cope with resistance to change—also known as resistance to your project's success. Here are some of the strategies available:

- Participation
- Communication
- Education
- Listening, supportive attitude
- Negotiation, compromise
- Manipulation
- Coercion

Let's examine what these approaches mean and how they work.

**Participation** means you involve the people who are resisting. You ask them to help develop and roll out the change. Who resists his/her own implementation plan? Or if your implementation plan is already in place, let the resisters shoot holes in it, tell you everything that is wrong with it—and then develop solutions to the problems they have identified. This will, at minimum, keep them busy, sate their destructive instincts and keep them out of your hair.

**Communication** helps prevent resistance. If you are communicating clearly and often, people will not be surprised by the change. They will have known for quite some time what the change is, why it is being implemented, what will happen and when. Does this sound like your project? Does every person who will be affected know *exactly* what to expect? If not, you need a better communication plan.

**Education** means that any changes to process, daily routine, communications or other work activities will be addressed in training. This might be traditional, instructor-led training in a classroom or it might be online or on-demand-via-mobile-device training. Non-traditional training might even include games; "gamification" of learning is not only fun, but people appear to learn more quickly and remember longer when they are enjoying themselves. Think creatively about education for your change project.

Sometimes all a person who is resisting needs is someone (specifically you, the project manager) to **listen** to his/her issues and show empathy. There may be nothing you can do to solve this person's problem, but sometimes just listening respectfully and conveying sincerely that you understand his or her distress can change that person's attitude and, more importantly, behavior. After all, it costs you no-thing to listen and you may be able to address their concerns later, since you are now aware of them.

Sometimes Department A wants the process to work *this* way, while Department B wants it to work *that* way. This is the point at which you put on your **negotiator** hat and start trying to broker a compromise. Perhaps you can find something in your project that one of the parties wants *even more* than they want their way on the current issue. If so, you may be able to hammer out a deal.

**Manipulating** sponsors, team members and stakeholders often works, but you would be playing with fire. People who are manipulated, and find out about it later, can be very vengeful. While many consultants opt for manipulation (consultants are, after all, smooth-talking and manipulative by nature), and even encourage their clients to do so, we believe this will come back to haunt you. If you feel tempted to use manipulation because you plan to leave this company and even the industry, remember: bad deeds will *always* follow you.

**Coercion** is, like manipulation, a slippery slope. If you force people to do things your way, on your schedule, you will find they will work twice as hard to get you back. Coercion, similar to confrontation in conflict resolution, is a "my way or the high way" game. People do not like being coerced and will plot your downfall, even if it takes them years. You really do not want to do this unless your back is against a wall. During a particularly difficult project, I indicated to the project sponsor that one department was still refusing to "sign off" on the application being implemented. She said, "Let me get my baseball bat and pay that department a visit." I asked her to let me try to negotiate a deal first, but to keep her bat at the ready in case I failed. Fortunately, I succeeded. Coercion should always be a last resort.

**Selecting a Strategy for Coping with Resistance**

The key to picking the right strategy is to know these things:

- who the stakeholders are, their habits, likes, dislikes, strengths, and weaknesses
- how the change will impact people and the way they work
- what people's assumptions and fears are
- what has worked in this organization before
- what resources are available
- how important this change will be to the organization

Once you are aware of these things, it is a simple matter of matching them to your coping strategies. Communication and education are always at the top of our list. Education addresses assumptions, fears and ignorance, while communication will take care of explaining what impact the change will have on people's daily routines. Knowing your resources will allow you to negotiate deals from a position of strength. Participation and listening are both free (except for the time you must invest) and we highly recommend them regardless of whether you identify specific requirements that indicate a need for them.

Of course if you already know what works in this organization, it is probably wise to start with that strategy. But if you come from the "outside" (i.e. you are a consultant), it may be difficult to determine what worked before as you will get a variety of conflicting stories from different people when you ask. If that is the case, just use logic and reason to select a strategy. No one will ever figure out how you did it

**Key Lessons**

There are five options for handling conflict: Confronting, Collaborating, Compromising, Avoiding and Accommodating.

Thoroughly document and track all project issues.

Make sure decision authority is clear by creating a Decision Authority Matrix.

Be sure to identify and involve all "interested parties" in issue resolution.

Communication, education and participation are the most effective strategies to address resistance to change. Manipulation and coercion are strategies to be used rarely, if at all.

## Chapter 5: Risk Management

*We were moving a data center. Not the easiest of tasks, but we had it all planned perfectly. We had purchased identical hardware and software so that there were duplicates of everything. No system would ever be down because we could still use the original system if the cutover did not work. We knew the dates the servers would cut over and we had the old and new data centers connected via "big pipes" (telecommunication lines).*

*We did have one major risk: one server was so old, it could not easily be replicated. But we checked with users and other stakeholders, and everyone agreed that the server could be down for about five days without impacting productivity, as long as it was up again on the sixth day.*

*The move plan had a 24-hour window: the vendor would shut down and pack the server, drive it to the staging warehouse at the airport, load it onto the plane, fly from California to Tennessee, unload and transport the server to the new data center, and bring it back up. There was a status call from the vendor after each step was completed. A one-day move plan within a five-day window seemed to give us a large margin to recover from any delay. We could even handle the unknown unknowns—or so we thought.*

*Then we got the call. "The Feds seized the warehouse where we were holding the server while waiting for the flight," said the voice on the phone. What? "Apparently they got an anonymous tip that a gun runner was storing arms there, so they came in and are not allowing anything to leave the warehouse."*

*So much for the large window. "How long will it take them to release the server to us?"*

*"They won't give us an answer. It could be weeks."*

*There are a lot of things you can plan for. But you cannot plan for the Feds seizing the warehouse.*

# Shifting Sands

## Chapter Summary

This chapter focuses on an area that is often neglected until it is too late: risk management. The techniques explored offer ways to plan for both conceivable disasters and unimaginable events.

Topics include how to evaluate contingencies, why binary triggers are essential and why bad news can sometimes be good news.

## Risk Management: Avoiding the Quicksand That Will Engulf Your Project

Projects never go according to plan. Murphy's Law ("Anything that can go wrong, will go wrong") is alive and well in the world of project management. Change happens. You can plan for it, you can be resilient and adaptable—or you can be caught off-guard. The former is preferable.

We talked about change management in an earlier chapter. The ability to handle and communicate change effectively is a key skill that helps ensure project success. While communicating a planned change may feel different than communicating a change that happened unexpectedly to the project, they don't have to be different. You should instead plan how you want to handle possible internal and external changes that may affect your project.

The original project plan rarely comes to fruition as designed. You'll find that the risk management plan saves your project from disaster. For that reason, you must continually keep an updated risk management plan as a key part of your project.

### What is risk?

Before going too deeply into this discussion, you may be wondering what, exactly, risk is. In its simplest form a risk is "something bad" that could happen to your project.

When creating a risk management plan, you will need these elements:

- Risk description: a clear statement describing the "bad thing" about which you are worried

- Impact: the negative effects of the risk (i.e., why you were worried in the first place)

- Likelihood: the probability this "bad thing" will happen (usually expressed as high, medium or low)

- Mitigation: steps to take to prevent the risk event from happening

- Trigger: objective event that indicates that the risk situation has happened and puts the contingency plan into action

- Contingency: steps to take after the risk situation has happened (workaround)

**Evaluate contingencies in terms of severity and probability**

The first—and most important—part of risk management is brainstorming possible problems, the potential impact of those problems, and the likelihood of the problems occurring. This process doesn't have to be too complex; high/medium/low is acceptable for both impact and likelihood. After the risks are brainstormed and evaluated, you should identify the top ten to worry about and decide what you're going to do about each risk.

Let's pick the simplest one for many project managers: the deliverables and timelines are the same, but your people resources are either redeployed or leave the organization. What are you going to do about it? The time to decide is at the beginning of the project, not when the problem arises. There are many questions that you should ask: What is the impact of losing resources? What is the likelihood of losing resources? How difficult (and expensive) would it be to hire or contract people with the right skills?

You should do likewise with changes in scope, especially scope creep. How are you going to handle requests for more deliverables or

Shifting Sands

more functionality? What is the impact? How likely is this? Do you need a change control board to get agreement from stakeholders? Again, the time to decide this is at the beginning of the project.

How about having the timelines moved? Is that a problem? Is that likely to happen?

Then start asking your team to help brainstorm what else can go wrong. In addition to the above—scope creep, lost resources, and compressed timelines—you may want to consider the following:

- What will the team do if the sponsor changes?
- What will the team do if the project manager (that's you!) is assigned to another project?
- For systems development projects, what will the team do if the technical lead leaves the project?
- What will the team do if additional funding becomes available?
- What will the team do if the project's sponsors don't like the deliverables?

You should establish how you will handle these risks long before the contingency becomes reality.

**Use binary automatic triggers**

Once you have identified the impact and likelihood of risks, as well as what to do about them, you need automatic triggers for those risks.

An automatic trigger takes the guesswork out of whether or not the risk has occurred. The trigger should be of a form that can be answered objectively as either true or false. For example, we have seen software projects that trigger on loss of 10% or more of the project's capital funding, with the contingency that the project will significantly reduce the software's functionality and pursue a previously identified alternative of an expenses-only approach.

**Have a mitigation strategy whenever possible**

Risk management is not just contingencies. Often, these scenarios can be addressed earlier in order to minimize the impact.

Every scenario should identify not just a contingency, but also a mitigation. For example, you may be concerned that your technical lead will leave the project, but you can minimize the impact of that happening by obtaining funding to cross-train an additional resource in case that person leaves.

And along those lines, every good risk management plan should not only identify the possible loss of the project manager as a risk, but also have a project management succession strategy as a mitigation.

To see how mitigations and contingencies are used on an actual project, consider the case where one of the authors was the technical architect for a critical infrastructure project. As such, the project identified the risk that the architect could leave the team. The risk plan identified how this scenario would be handled. The mitigation was that the project should acquire and cross-train an additional resource. The contingency was that, should the architect leave the team, the project would be delayed six months while new team members were brought up to speed. Unfortunately, funding challenges prevented the additional resource from being hired, so the risk was accepted with just the contingency. When the architect was promoted, the project team responded according to the plan: all phases were automatically pushed back six months. Nobody asked why. Everyone—including the project sponsor—already knew the specific response for this situation that was provided in the project's risk plan.

**Insist on receiving bad news early**

## Shifting Sands

We have already talked about communication, but when managing risks, it is imperative that you receive bad news as quickly as possible. When you receive bad news, be extremely thankful that you are hearing it now and not when it is too late to do anything about it.

The 1-10-100 rule of software development sums up this situation well: a problem takes ten times the effort to fix in the development phase vs. the design phase, and takes one hundred times the effort if fixed in the testing phase. And the cost to fix it after the software is "in the field" is astronomical. Our experience is that this software-development rule applies across all types of projects, not just systems-development projects.

*As an example, consider this case: Long ago, when client/server was the hot technology, there was client-based software which helped customers order items. The client tool—what the customer saw—had one small bug: when the server was down, the software reported an error: "Error #4." The software should have said "The server is down; please try again in 5 minutes," or something to that effect, since this server's outages were rare and usually lasted no more than a few minutes.*

*So how big of a deal was this?*

*If the developer had found the problem, the bug could have been fixed in less than a minute.*

*If the team had raised the issue prior to the product's release, the bug could have been fixed and regression tested in an hour.*

*Instead, the team found the problem after the software was in customers' hands and they had only two choices:*

- *update the software and send new disks to the customers (which would have cost about $10,000) or*
- *leave the bug*

*The team chose to leave the bug since the server was rarely down. The team later regretted that decision when, due to a network error, the server was not accessible for several hours. All the customers who received the error called the Customer Service line and pressed 4, which unfortunately put them in touch with the only group that had not been trained to help them. Ouch!*

Only when you receive the bad news early do you have the luxury of choosing from many options to resolve the problem.

**Reevaluate the risk plan regularly**

There are always things you won't know, the unknown unknowns. You cannot plan for the Feds seizing the warehouse. But you can reevaluate the risk plan regularly to determine which of the unknown unknowns are now known, and which may be worth worrying about.

Take the example at the beginning of the chapter: Even in the next plan, you probably would not plan for the warehouse being locked down. But you would want to begin worrying about what might happen if that server doesn't come up. What if it's lost by the airline? What if it gets doused by a sprinkler system? What if it is delayed beyond five days for any number of reasons? The project had a plan in case of destruction of the server, but not for its delay.

A lengthy delay of a perfectly working server was never considered of sufficient likelihood to cause worry. But once the server was seized, the team saw the gaping hole in the risk plan. The first response was a mitigation: find someone who might be able to negotiate the release of the server.

**Conclusion—What Happened**

*Wondering what happened to that server that we mentioned at the beginning of this chapter?*

## Shifting Sands

*Fortunately, our vendor had been heavily involved in the project from the beginning. And as it turned out, that vendor also had a strong relationship with this federal agency (the agency was also a client). The vendor explained the situation and vouched for the integrity of the server, providing the project plan which verified the server had never been out of the possession of the vendor. The federal authorities released the server the next day, well within our five day window.*

*As a footnote: Once the server arrived and was "stood up," the Director of Systems Engineering came by our office to share the good news. Then he casually said, "By the way, what should I do with all the AK-47's that were inside the server case?" Everyone is a comic.*

**Key Lessons**

Make a detailed risk plan prioritized by the probability and severity of impact any event might have.

Create and use automatic binary triggers to reduce the complexity of deciding whether to invoke a contingency or mitigation plan.

Have a mitigation plan whenever possible (to avoid actually triggering the contingency plan).

Look for bad news; it is important that you find out about problems sooner rather than later. Reward your team when they come to you and share potential problems as soon as they surface.

## Chapter 6: Metrics

*Once upon a time, there was a phenomenally successful project.*

*We know it was a phenomenally successful project because the project manager told us so.*

*And it's a good thing this project was so successful. The project was one of the largest and most critical in the company's history. This software would affect thousands of users inside the company and could ultimately impact external customers as well. It was critical to hit all of the dates. Everything had to be perfect.*

*Measuring every aspect of the project—from the number of requirements successfully written to the progress of every single task—the project manager assured us that the project was well ahead of schedule. The metrics proved it: while a handful of tasks may have missed the schedule slightly, almost all of the tasks were already 80%-90% complete, and there should be no problem making up any lost time.*

*The project manager was slightly overoptimistic. Two weeks before the delivery date, the project manager awkwardly announced that the phenomenally successful project would be delayed. As it turned out, the delay was longer than the original timeline.*

*If only the project manager had known that there is a people side to metrics.*

**Chapter Summary**

Establishing metrics can be daunting, so we have provided guidelines to help the project manager select the right things to measure. Unfortunately, measuring too many things can prove as damaging as not measuring anything.

Key concepts include binary deliverables, where to obtain estimates, which issues to log and when to trust instincts over numbers.

## Measure Twice, Cut Once—Without Measuring Every Grain of Sand

The previous chapters have talked about the people side of project management. How involving, motivating, and satisfying the correct people will help ensure a successful plan. How influencing and credibility are critical. How change management and communications keep everyone informed. How conflict resolution ensures that issues are addressed promptly and effectively. How risk management ensures that the team is prepared for whatever might happen.

Finally, we turn to metrics. For those of us who have a slight quantitative tilt, metrics provide comfort due to their impartiality, reliability, and invulnerability.

*Wrong.* As with the rest of this book, there is a people side to metrics. How you establish, track, and respond to metrics is often the difference between a successful project and that awkward delay that has everyone wondering what went wrong.

Within the woodworking community, there is an old saw, so to speak, about how you should "measure twice, cut once." Think about it: if measurements are always the same, then why would you measure twice? Because sometimes you get a different answer.

Your project can also tell different stories, depending on the metrics you establish and track.

## Deliverables Are Binary

In "Twelve Keys to Successful Software Development" (found in the Appendix ), we note that the first 90% of the project takes 10% of the time, while the other 10% of the project takes the other 90% of the time.

It's easy to estimate that a task is 90% complete, especially when that unit of work should take only a couple of days. The problem is that, even when that number is in line with that task's deliverable, it's in line only because of the human tendency to grab the low-hanging fruit first. Therefore, percentage-based task progress—and by association project progress—will usually soar to 75% to 90% complete, then remain there while everyone figures out how to accomplish the last 10 to 25%. Getting that last 10% can often take as long as getting the first 90%.

The Agile Development software community has the answer to this problem, with its principle that you measure progress by measuring working software.

This is what we call a binary metric for a deliverable.

You may recall learning about binary numbers, where the only numerals are one (1) or zero (0). So decimal 2 is binary 10, and decimal 75 is binary 1001011. Everything is described as a combination of 1 and 0.

Your project management metrics should be the same way. Either the task is done or it is not. It is 100% complete or it is 0%. Likewise, each deliverable is 100% or 0%.

Feel free to break down the tasks and deliverables into whatever components you think are worth measuring. Just remember that either they're done or they're not. That's the concept of binary metrics for deliverables.

**Risk triggers should use binary metrics for deliverables, attached to objective dates**

The National Transportation Safety Board, when investigating private-plane incidents, has found that a disproportionate number of crashes appear to be caused by the Almost There Syndrome. This happens when a pilot prepares a plan for a contingency, but does not follow the plan. "Yes, I am a little lower on fuel than I thought—and yes, I'm below the threshold where I said I would turn toward my alternate airport. But I'm almost there: I can see my destination." Within the private-plane aviation industry, this thinking often leads to disaster. (Fortunately, professional pilots are well-trained to follow the contingency plans *every* time.)

The decisions you make on your project may not be as life-and-death as the decisions a pilot must make. Nevertheless, there is a lesson to be learned.

Binary metrics for deliverables make risk management much simpler. All that you have to do is prepare the risk triggers in the following form: if this deliverable doesn't happen by that date, then here's what we're going to do about it on that date.

That's it. There is no room for Almost Done. There is no room for Just One Day More. Better to kick off the contingency than to wait for a task that never finishes.

On a personal note, one of us once self-assigned a critical software deliverable for a project. Then we designed an extremely complex model for the software that would greatly improve the project's analytical capabilities. The alternative was to use an expensive off-the-shelf software package that didn't have close to the same functionality. If the custom-designed deliverable didn't happen, then the project needed the alternative, because without either, the project would definitely fail.

So what did we do? We self-assigned the tasks, but we also chose a trusted project manager to track us. "If I don't have this done by this date, here's what you must do," we said. "Do not accept any excuses—as Nike says, 'Just Do It.'"

When the date rolled around, guess who didn't have the deliverable ready? (Sad, but true.) We were close—really close—and we pleaded our case. And the risk manager wisely quoted our instructions back to us and triggered the contingency. The contingency was executed, it worked, and we cleared the final hurdle.

By the way, we never did finish writing the custom software. The risk manager did the right thing.

Do yourself the favor of ensuring that your risk management triggers use binary deliverables and objective dates. You'll thank us later.

**Estimates Are Usually Reliable—Except Estimates of Availability**

While deliverable metrics may be binary, that is not the case for the estimates of how much effort is required to accomplish that task.

The research on project estimation shows it is not uncommon for estimates to be off by 100%. Yet our experience shows that estimates tend to be really reliable. We have several years of data on estimates-vs-actuals, and we find that the estimates of how many hours will be required to complete a task or deliverable are usually within 20% of the hours projected.

If that is the case, why does the project take twice as long? The reason is that the estimator thought there were eight hours in a workday. It's more common to have only two to four *available* hours in a workday.

If you're like us, you have been to your share of staff meetings, project meetings, status meetings, all-hands meetings, information sessions, town halls and training classes. There are also tasks such as administrative paperwork, things that will "only take a minute," and relationship building, all of which take time that is never in the project plan. Of course, none of this takes into account vacation or illness. Considering all of these time pits, how could anyone assume that there are eight available hours in a workday?

In the project world, four hours of productive work a day is a huge accomplishment. And in the software-design world, two hours a day is much more likely.

While we are on the topic, on our projects, for those time periods when a third or more of the participants are out of the office (e.g., the week between Christmas and New Year's), our project plans assume that no work happens that week. The reason is that any project team member who is in the office will invariably need the help of someone who is out of the office, so most tasks will have to wait until other people return.

**Celebrate bad news by logging its existence and what you did about it**

We have been on project teams that never made a mistake, at least according to the problem logs. Every deliverable was there; every date was met. Sure, the users hate the system, but the solution was delivered, and that's the important thing.

We have also been on project teams that logged and discussed so many errors that it was embarrassing. To be part of such an error-prone mess was definitely not cool; instead, you found yourself discussing problems, developing proposed solutions, prioritizing fixes, and validating both deliverables and bug fixes.

Guess which teams had the successful projects? Yes, the second group: the group that insisted on logging every issue, regardless of how small.

When you receive issues, log them. Then figure out what to do about them. Address the issues with the team and collectively figure out what to do about the issues. When you're addressing the issues, be sure to ask what impact the proposed resolution has on the scope, the resource consumption, and the timelines. Anything that has a minor impact should be able to move ahead. In those cases document the proposed resolution and when that resolution is expected. Then track it until it is closed, or until a different resolution presents itself.

And while you're determining resolutions, for future reference it may help to identify which are design changes vs. which are implementation fixes. Was the original design flawed? If we make this change, does it impact other parts of the project? For implementation fixes, usually the scope is narrowed to that feature itself (which is why it's often good to distinguish between design and implementation).

Some problems may not even be problems; they may be previously identified issues, in which case cross-reference the previous issue, and if the previous issue is still open, then close the new issue.

Logging the issues is not the same as fixing every problem immediately. There are times when you find that a problem is too big to address within the original timeframes, or the problem, while worth solving, turned out to be outside the original scope. For those occasions, you must talk to your stakeholders and jointly determine the best resolution. You can delete the requirement, defer the requirement, or add sufficient resources to deliver the requirement without impacting the rest of the project.

So celebrate when you receive bad news early, and reinforce to your team that communication is key to the project's success.

**If it doesn't look right, it probably isn't**

The last lesson for metrics has to do with how you handle the information you collect. You have broken down the deliverables to a granular level of binary tasks, you have developed estimates on how long to do those tasks, and you are tracking actuals against those estimates.

Your automatic triggers will handle the most severe risks that you identify. But the best project managers don't wait. They analyze the metrics to see if anything looks amiss before the contingency even kicks in—possibly driving changes to the contingency plan.

If the status remains the same but you don't know why, ask. If estimates are tracking significantly longer—or even shorter—than expected, dig a little deeper to understand the causes. If issues are not being raised, find out the reasons.

The best project managers take that extra step to understand the dynamics of the project and modify their contingency plans accordingly.

## Conclusion: What Happened

*In the example that begins this chapter, the project manager should have known that something was wrong when the task deliverables stayed at the same completion level over a period of several weeks. Yes, the deliverables were still ahead of plan, even considering the poorly designed metrics for project progress. Yet the metrics were not moving anymore and nobody was bringing up any issues.*

*In short, it didn't look right. The project manager suspected something might be wrong, but did not act on that suspicion. The project manager compounded the problem by not following the contingency plans since everyone was so close to being finished.*

*As it turned out, resources were being reallocated, but nobody wanted to give the bad news to the project manager. You can see how following the metrics lessons above would have lowered the risk to that project.*

## Key Lessons

Only measure those things which are critical to the project's success, and make the measurement binary. A task is either done by a specific date, or it is not; there is no 90% complete.

Use binary triggers to invoke the risk plan for tasks not complete by due date.

When you get bad news, determine whether you have a design or implementation problem—and whether it is in scope to be fixed during the project timeline.

If something does not look right, it probably isn't. Dig more deeply into things that don't look or feel quite right. It is better to be over-vigilant than blindsided.

# Chapter 7: Don't Go It Alone

"Never tell people how to do things. Tell them what to do and they will surprise you with their ingenuity."

—*General George Smith Patton, Jr.*

*During an engagement to implement an enterprise-wide application, we had a severe software problem. Although the problem had been reported through the normal channels, the vendor's turnaround time for fixing what they considered a non-critical problem was a month. We needed the fix in no more than two weeks. Because the project sponsor had agreed to be a reference account for the vendor and had hosted multiple potential clients, she was able to call in a favor and get the vendor to send a developer from headquarters to fix the code onsite. This favor kept us on schedule and moving forward.*

## Chapter Summary

While the project manager is certainly where "the buck stops," others can help with communications, politics, relationships and problem-solving, but you do have to ask for their help. And when we say "others," we mean both inside and outside of the organization for which you are managing the project (whether that is your employer or your client). We also mean those above you and your peers, in addition to your project team members.

Key concepts include delegating upward, getting input from a diverse group, clarifying between "this would be nice" and "this is a hard and fast constraint."

## The Role of Sponsors, Team Members and Others in Project Management

*Many years into my project management experience I was talking to someone about "my project" when I realized, it isn't really my project; it is the organization's project. As project manager I am tasked with directing work on the project, but that does not mean that*

*I personally have to do every task. Of course, I understood how to assign technical tasks, but it had escaped me that the "people side" tasks were just as assignable as the technical tasks (almost).*

*Once I realized that tasks were tasks, regardless of their nature, I began appointing team members and sponsors as "owners" of relationships. Owners reported on their relationship status and events affecting the relationship, just as they reported on any other project task, but in one-on-one meetings rather than in the full project team meetings in deference to the delicate nature of the information.*

\*\*\*\*\*\*\*\*\*\*\*\*\*\*\*\*\*\*\*\*\*\*\*\*\*\*\*\*\*\*\*\*\*\*\*\*\*\*\*\*\*\*\*\*\*\*\*\*\*\*\*\*\*\*\*\*\*\*\*\*

Sometimes as a project manager it feels as though the weight of the world is on your shoulders. If the project fails (or is late, over budget or doesn't deliver every promised result) that somehow is your personal failure to own and be miserable about.

But let's stop and think. There are probably dozens, or for large projects even hundreds, of people assigned to this project; why are you the only accountable person? Perhaps it's because you have chosen to be; you have somehow tacitly agreed to take all blame. And everyone is happy for the project manager to take the blame for any problems, delays, mistakes or failures. But be assured everyone will bask in the glow of success if the project blows its goals out of the water.

We point out this lack of accountability on project teams because spreading responsibility and accountability for non-technical tasks across team members, sponsors, vendors and others has more to do with the mindset of the project manager than with the nature of the tasks. Are you, the project manager, able to accept work that is sufficient, but possibly below the quality level you would accomplish yourself? Are you willing to coach and guide others in managing a relationship, navigating politics or crafting communications when it might be faster to do it yourself? Are you willing to take the risk that the relationships, communications and problem-solving you assign to others will not be done on time and to your standards?

Certainly you have made this mental leap on technical tasks. Even if a technical task is in your specialty area, the most involved you, as a

project manager, would become is reviewing it closely to see that it has been done to your standards. Why are the "people side" tasks any different? Why is it harder to let go of them?

Because relationships are part of your persona (i.e. everyone you know is part of who you are), it is difficult to assign what you may feel is "part of you" to someone else. However, learning to assign these non-technical tasks is essential to surviving many years of project management without losing your mind. For best results and maximum retention of sanity, we recommend you start now.

**Sponsors**

Project sponsors are usually fairly high level executives. They have gotten where they are by understanding the organization's politics and managing relationships (and one hopes also because they have good business skills).

Sponsors should be very open to discussing the people side of the project, and it is important that you start these discussions and set sponsors' expectations as early as possible in the project.

Sponsors will expect (or should expect) to own many relationships that are key to the project's success. However, you should be pro-active and discuss with the sponsor(s) exactly what help you want and need long before you need it. Ask the sponsor to explain which of the key executives in the organization are supportive of the project and which are lukewarm or even against it. Ask for best case and worst case scenarios for the project. What could happen that would be disastrous? What could happen that would make this the greatest project you have ever run?

Once you understand the possible scenarios, ask for clarification on what parts of the scope, objectives and resources assigned are guidelines and what is a hard constraint (for example, if we find we need a little more time to do things right, can we ask to extend the deadline, or is this project's deadline a "drop dead" date? Are there financial or legal consequences to missing the date?). What you may have thought were hard constraints could just be the sponsor's first guess at the time and resources the project will need. Sometimes sponsors are happy to go back to the well to get additional resources or more time if they feel that is what is needed to do the job right. But you will never know if you don't ask.

The next discussion with the sponsor(s) should be about problem solving. Clearly, you know where to find the technical problem-solvers, both on staff and from vendors/service providers. But what happens if the problem is political? Who can help you (and the sponsor) with that? What resources are available? Who are the sponsor's mentors, allies and supporters? What parts of the project are likely to spark a political response?

Then ask about resources. What money, people, vendors and favors can the sponsor provide if he/she has to? Sometimes the success of a project rests on calling in favors. Such a case is described in the opening vignette when a vendor flew a developer from their headquarters to the client's site to fix a code problem as a favor to the sponsor.

Next you need to assess the sponsor's communication skills. Does the sponsor have the presentation skills to run a town hall meeting? Does he/she give inspirational, convincing pitches or does someone on the sponsor's staff need to give those presentations? You should play to the strengths of your sponsor, but also recognize his or her limitations. If you need to skew the communications plan more to written emails and newsletter articles, it's better to know that in the planning stage than after the first abysmal in-person presentation.

Finally, you need to know what relationships the sponsor has outside the organization that might help the project. For example, does this sponsor interact with external customers of the organization? If so, can the outside customers be helpful in making it clear to internal people that this project is benefiting the customer and making him/her happy, and therefore the employees need to endure the pain of change for the customer's sake? Does this sponsor know vendors who could be of assistance? Sometimes projects need a specific skill that is not on staff and not available through other vendors already working on the project. It would be nice if the project manager knew which vendors the sponsor could call with very little notice and negotiate a great price for a needed skill.

Sponsors can, and should, be active participants in the project. They should assume responsibility for many relationships, help manage vendors, connect the project manager to needed resources and help solve problems. Be sure to discuss all of these topics and make appropriate assessments of the sponsor's skills and resources very early in the project. Never hesitate to delegate upwards to get important relationships, political issues and other non-technical tasks handled by your sponsor(s).

Most of all set your sponsor's expectations correctly and establish good communications. Sponsors obviously want the project to succeed—it affects their careers as much as, if not more than, it affects yours. Be sure to align your goals with the sponsor's and understand your sponsor's skills, resources and connections.

**Team Members**

Project managers often tell me they have X number of full-time resources and Y number of part-time resources. Please understand that none of your resources are "full time." As pointed out in previous chapters, no one has forty hours a week to allocate to the project. We all know there is some amount of administrative overhead as well as time away from work, but there is also the "I just need this person for two days" issue.

No matter who your assigned resources are, they will inevitably be temporarily pulled off the project at the exact moment when you need 110% of their time. It's Murphy's Law and it has never been more robustly present than it is today in our "do more with less" business culture.

Despite their part-time status, team members are often the right ones to "own" relationships. If you are an outside consultant, or even an employee, but have never worked with the people involved in and affected by this particular project, you need the help of team members who have known the stakeholders longer. At one engagement I needed to influence and get buy-in from managers in the field. One of my team members had been working with these managers for many years through a number of different roles during her rise in the organization. Who would get better responses from these managers—an outside consultant whom they had just met, or a trusted internal person with whom they had worked for years? The answer is obvious and so was who should "own" those relationships and be responsible for influencing the managers. Choices for relationship ownership are not always this obvious, but you should at least analyze each stakeholder group and decide who makes the best relationship manager. No stakeholder group should be without a relationship owner, even if they are clearly pro-project. Every group needs an "inside person" on the project team to whom they can go for information, advice and advocacy.

Sometimes what you need from team members is for them to help each other complete tasks—even if the task at hand is not officially in the domain of the person helping. For example, if the team member writing newsletter articles, memos and other communications is falling behind and you have another team member who has good writing skills and some free time (despite his/her being a network engineer or some other technical staff), wouldn't it be nice if the skilled person with extra time would pitch in and help the beleaguered communications staffer?

The way you get this altruistic behavior to happen is by making clear to the team that everyone sinks or swims together. The goals of the team *must* be shared; everyone must feel compelled to help other team members whom they see struggling. A mindset of "I've finished my tasks; too bad if others are behind on theirs" will not produce a successful project—or even a team. Teams pull together, collaborate, communicate and share goals, by definition. As project manager one of your most important tasks is to build your group of task-executers into an actual team.

To enable team members to help one another the project manager should try to discover as many of each team member's skills as possible. Even if you have a copy of a team member's job description and performance appraisal (which is highly unlikely unless the team member is your direct report), you probably don't know about all of their skills. In a casual, social environment (over lunch or coffee, while bowling etc.) talk to each team member and get to know him/her as a person. Where are they from, what are their degrees in, what other jobs have they had, where have they lived, what other industries have they worked in? If your network engineer has an undergrad degree in journalism, it's a good bet he/she can write. You won't know that unless you ask the sort of open-ended, curious questions that lead you to each person's hidden skills. Of course sometimes it is easier than this; you come into a department and everyone tells you that Judy's non-technical skill is graphic design. You now know who on the team can create any needed graphical materials—brochures, posters, newsletters or screen designs.

Facilitating communication between team members is another task for which the project manager is responsible. Does everyone on the team know what everyone else on the team is working on? Do they all know the status of every work stream in the project? Do they know where they could help, if they have the right skills and the time? Part of getting people to help one another is letting them know when some part of the project needs help. As project manager you have the broadest view of how things are going, and you need to be sure everyone has access to your view.

## Unaffiliated Parties

Sometimes there are family members, friends, colleagues in professional organizations or even "virtual" colleagues (e.g., the ones you converse with in LinkedIn Groups or Facebook Groups) who might be able to offer advice or help when a project is having difficulty.

Again, you will never know what your friends, relatives and colleagues know or how they can help you if you don't tell them what is going on and ask for their advice, help or suggestions. Crowdsourcing solutions is a widely approved current concept, but people with good communications skills and broad social networks (the person-to-person kind that pre-pre-dated online social networks) have been crowdsourcing for decades. Computers and social media make crowdsourcing much easier, but the concept is not a recent invention.

If you are facing a problem, go to a professional organization meeting and ask for help (in terms that don't let confidential information or details become public). For project managers that organization might be PMI, an industry organization or some other topic-specific organization. If those meetings are not easily accessible, try a special-interest LinkedIn Group. The ideas offered might not solve your problem, but they might make you think of something else that will.

Looking for inspiration outside of the organization, outside of the industry or outside of the country is a wise move. Seeking diverse views and broad input is always good—assuming you have the time to do this and synthesize the results into something helpful. If time is tight, seek out an expert in solving this particular type of problem. The solution may be less innovative, but if you need a solution quickly, this ordinary solution might have to do.

## Key Lessons

### General

Delegate or assign non-technical tasks including relationship management, political maneuvering and solving non-technical problems.

### Sponsors

Set expectations and develop strong, ongoing communications.

Determine all skills, resources and connections the sponsor(s) can provide to help the project, whether the resources are inside the organization or external.

## Team Members

Determine which team members should "own" relationships, problem-solving and other non-technical tasks.

Find out all of your team members' "secret skills," the ones that are not obvious from their job titles.

Facilitate communications and shared goals between team members

Be sure every team member knows what is happening in all parts of the project and is pitching in to help where possible

## Unaffiliated Parties

Seek broad, diverse input when solving problems—from outside the organization, outside the industry and from industry and professional organization colleagues. There is always more than one right answer to a problem; be sure you look beyond the first solution you stumble upon. Evaluate the long-term impact of the solutions from which you choose.

# Appendix A

Recommended Reading List

Bridges, William and Susan Bridges. *Managing Transitions: Making the Most of Change*, Perseus Books Group, 2009.

Kotter, John P. *Leading Change*. Harvard Business Press, 1996.

Kotter, John P. and Lorne A. Whitehead. *buy\*in: saving your good idea from getting shot down*. Harvard Business Review Press, 2010.

Kouzes, James and Barry Z. Posner. *Credibility: How Leaders Gain and Lose IT, Why People Demand IT*. Jossey-Bass, 2003.

Patterson, Kerry, et al. *Crucial Conversations: Tools for talking when stakes are high,* McGraw-Hill, 2002.

Patterson, Kerry, et al. *Influencer: The Power to Change Anything,* McGraw-Hill, 2008.

Thomas, Kenneth W. *Introduction to Conflict Management*, CPP, Inc., 2002.

# Appendix B

## Twelve Keys to Successful Software Development

1. **COMMUNICATE EARLY AND OFTEN!**
   Communicate as early as possible, especially bad news. You can solve just about any problem if you identify and communicate issues early in the development process. But if you wait until late in the development process, those same problems will be very difficult and costly. Work to create an environment where people are comfortable communicating problems. If you are managing the project effectively, you should be hearing bad news on a regular basis.

2. **ENCOURAGE QUESTIONS – EVEN WHEN THE ANSWER APPEARS OBVIOUS.**
   The only stupid question is the one you were afraid to ask. Make the effort to understand the issues. Ask the stupid questions. Challenge the assumptions. Listen to the answers.

3. **SHARE THE GLORY AND TAKE THE BLAME.**
   Believe in the team, publicize the victories, and protect the team when problems arise. If the news is good, find a way to share the benefits. If the news is bad, take the blame yourself.

4. **DO YOUR ANALYSIS AND THINK SHORT-TERM.**
   Few software projects should ever take longer than six months to analyze, code, design, and test. The easiest way to shorten the development time is to add more analysis to the beginning of the project. If your development schedule remains longer than six months, then break the project down into six-month sub-projects and concentrate on the first six months to keep the team and stakeholders motivated.

5. **HOPE FOR THE BEST, AND PREPARE FOR THE WORST.**
   Every software project needs a certain amount of optimism in order to keep the momentum going. Yet each software project also needs a solid contingency plan, preferably taking into account the greatest values within a likelihood-by-impact matrix and including automatic triggers that define when the execute each contingency. After the quality of communications, the greatest factor in the success of any given software-development project is the quality of the *contingency* plan, *not* the quality of the original plan.

6. **PROTOTYPE TO PRODUCTION.**
   A picture is worth a thousand words. Therefore, draw pictures. Prototype as much functionality as is reasonably possible. Prototype early in the development cycle, and get feedback from the all of the stakeholders. Then

# Shifting Sands

prototype and get feedback again. Continue this process until you receive the alpha test version of the software.

7. **MAKE USE OF USABILITY.**
Show the prototype to customers within a controlled usability lab environment, early in the development cycle. And remember to tell the customer *what* to do, not *how* to do it. What is intuitive to the developer often isn't intuitive to the customer.

8. **MAKE DECISIONS QUICKLY. STICK TO THEM! AND BE FLEXIBLE!**
Often it doesn't matter what the decision is, only that there is a decision. Make decisions quickly, and be prepared to defend them. Yet just because a decision has been made doesn't mean it's the right decision. If there's a compelling reason to change direction, then change it, preferably as early as possible. Each change in direction will add back an average of 50% of your consumed development time.

9. **REMEMBER THE 90/90 RULE OF SOFTWARE DEVELOPMENT.**
The 90/90 rule says that the first 90% of development takes 90% of the time, while the remaining 10% of development takes the other 90% of the time! This is because the easiest tasks are often completed first. Therefore, double all development schedules.

10. **REMEMBER THAT $T=(D-4)^2$.**
The amount of time that a software project will consume is proportional to the square of the number of developers, less four. In other words, never use more than four developers for any project. The more developers you have, the greater the potential for miscommunication.

11. **NEVER TRUST A FRIEND.**
Nothing against friends, but occasionally a friend has been known to take advantage of a friendship. Don't let that happen to you. Ensure alternate, trustworthy sources of information about your friend's performance. And remember that if it smells fishy, it's probably fish — even if your friend is the one holding the fish.

12. **REMEMBER THE PRESIDENT'S RULE.**
Better that your company president find a problem than that a customer find the same problem. Distribute your alpha and beta versions as widely as possible.

# Shifting Sands